MW00606943

Elite • 185

European Medieval Tactics (1)

The Fall and Rise of Cavalry 450–1260

DAVID NICOLLE

ILLUSTRATED BY ADAM HOOK
Series editor Martin Windrow

First published in Great Britain in 2011 by Osprey Publishing,
Midland House, West Way, Botley, Oxford, OX2 0PH, UK
44-02 23rd Street, Suite 219, Long Island City, NY 11101, USA
E-mail: info@ospreypublishing.com

A CIP catalogue record for this book is available from the British Library

Print ISBN: 978 1 84908 503 8
PDF e-book ISBN: 978 1 84908 504 5

David Nicolle has asserted his right under the Copyright, Designs and
Patents Act, 1988, to be identified as the Author of this Work.

Editor: Martin Windrow
Page layout: Ken Vail Graphic Design, Cambridge, UK (kvgd.com)
Index by Sandra Shotter
Typeset in Sabon and Myriad Pro
Originated by PDQ Digital Media Solutions, Suffolk, UK
Printed in China through Worldprint Ltd.

11 12 13 14 15   10 9 8 7 6 5 4 3 2 1

Osprey Publishing is supporting the Woodland Trust, the UK's leading
woodland conservation charity, by funding the dedication of trees.

www.ospreypublishing.com

DEDICATION

This one's for Charlie France, never properly appreciated

ARTIST'S NOTE

Readers may care to note that the original paintings from which the colour
plates in this book were prepared are available for private sale. All
reproduction copyright whatsoever is retained by the Publishers. All
enquiries should be addressed to:

Scorpio Gallery, PO Box 475, Hailsham, East Sussex BN27 2SL, UK

The Publishers regret that they can enter into no correspondence upon this
matter.

Title page: The battle scenes in the mid 13th-century French
Maciejowski Bible are not only finely detailed but also unflinchingly
gruesome, and probably reflect the reality of medieval warfare.
Here, mail-clad knights wield both swords and lances – note the
two-handed grip – to slay fleeing enemies, and are closely
supported by infantry with pole-arms. ('Defeat of the Moabites',
Pierpont Morgan Library, Ms. M. 638, f.12r, New York)

CONTENTS

INTRODUCTION   4

THE LATE ROMAN BACKGROUND   5

The 4th to mid 5th centuries . The *Notitia Dignitatum* . The aftermath of collapse in the West

THE AGE OF MIGRATIONS   10

Cavalry in the later 5th to 7th centuries: Romano-Byzantine armies . The steppe peoples . Germanic armies . Post-Roman Britain . Fighting on horseback
Infantry in the later 5th to 9th centuries: Romano-Byzantine manuals . Wagons as field fortifications . Styles of combat – the shield . The crossbow enigma

EARLY MEDIEVAL CAVALRY & INFANTRY   24

The 7th to early 10th centuries: Horse-harness and armour . Motivation and tactics . Equipment – archery

CAVALRY & CASTLES   33

The mid 10th to 11th centuries: Carolingian and Ottonian armies . Italy . Eastern and Central Europe . Northern Europe . The Iberian peninsula . Normans and French . The crossbow

THE SUPPOSED DOMINANCE OF CAVALRY   42

The 12th to mid 13th centuries: The Franco-Norman heartland . The border regions
Cavalry/infantry combinations: Light and heavy infantry . Italian militias . Archery . Anglo-Norman armies . Northern and Eastern Europe . The Celtic fringes

WARFARE AGAINST EXTERNAL ENEMIES   55

The Iberian peninsula . Crusader armies

BIBLIOGRAPHY   62

INDEX   64

EUROPEAN MEDIEVAL TACTICS (1)
THE FALL AND RISE OF CAVALRY,
AD 450–1260

INTRODUCTION

In the mid 12th century, the first place in Western Europe where fully enclosed helmets appeared, in conjunction with long mail *hauberks*, was the Iberian peninsula. ('Massacre of the Innocents', carved capital from Aquilar del Campo; Museo Arqueológico, Madrid)

The Early Medieval period saw the foundations of a new European civilization being laid, and alongside the emergence of new states came new military systems. These were partly the product of, and partly responsible for, new strategies, new tactics and modes of combat, and new attitudes towards warfare. The medieval period was probably more influential in the development of modern Europe than were the distant but generally more admired Classical civilizations of the ancient world.

A somewhat blinkered view of the European past, which focuses upon those essentially Mediterranean cultures, has been largely responsible for the concept of a supposedly distinctive 'Western way of warfare', which many still place in contrast to supposedly 'non-Western' practices. Such distinctions are largely fictitious, but they nevertheless reflect attitudes towards warfare within Western culture. There is a Western self-image of a civilization that fundamentally abhors war, and thus seeks to end it as quickly as possible by seeking a major and deciding confrontation. Taken to its extreme, this peculiar self-image proposes the superiority of heroic, face-to-face combat, preferably with close-quarter weapons. Largely fictitious as this picture may be, it nevertheless had a profound impact upon the development in medieval Western Europe of a civilization that was remarkable for its vigour, confidence and aggression, and which would, in time, project its influence and its military power into every corner of the world. Its prospects did not, however, look so promising following the collapse of the western half of the Roman Empire in the 5th century AD.

Although Western Christendom had regained some of its economic and military strength by the 8th century, its first phase of expansion was 'internal', in the sense that it was directed against those parts of the continent that were not yet Christian – most notably Germany and other parts of Central Europe (the subsequent 'conquest' of Scandiavia would be

Fighting on horseback, 12th century: a fleeing horseman vainly attempts to keep his pursuer at bay by thrusting his lance backwards. Both wear mail armour, the pursuer with a crown, the other rider apparently with a fluted helmet. In every kind of battlefield scenario, the greatest casualties were inflicted not in the head-on clash, but when a formation or group broke up and turned to flee. (*in situ* Cathedral, Angoulême; author's photograph)

cultural rather than military). Western Europe's first aggressive thrusts outwards would really begin in the 11th century, with the Iberian *Reconquista*, the German *Zug nach dem Osten* or expansion eastwards into previously pagan Slav lands, and the Norman conquest of Muslim-ruled Sicily. These initiatives were soon followed by crusades against both the Muslim peoples of the Middle East, and pagan eastern Baltic and Finnic peoples. These in turn were followed by so-called crusades against Orthodox fellow Christians in the Byzantine Empire, the Balkans and Russia, as well as against perceived heretics within Latin-Catholic Western Europe.

With the exception of warfare against internal heretics – which was much like European dynastic or proto-national struggles – most such campaigns pitted what might in simple terms be called 'Western warriors' against enemies with more or less different military traditions. Such differences should not, however, be exaggerated; in almost all cases – with the notable exception of the Finno-Ugrian and Turco-Mongol steppe peoples who invaded Europe from the east – the similarities between Western warriors and their varied opponents were much greater than the differences. This was as true of their strategies and tactics as it was of their military equipment, and even their personal motivations for combat. Despite the dramatic exceptions, most of Europe's military efforts continued to be directed inwards throughout the medieval period, and the so-called 'Triumph of the West' was a clearly post-medieval phenomenon. On the other hand, when this success was achieved, its initial phases were clearly built upon socio-military systems that had developed during medieval Europe's seemingly endless internal conflicts.

THE LATE ROMAN BACKGROUND

The 4th to mid 5th centuries
The tumultuous centuries that saw the collapse of the western half of the Roman Empire are widely known as the Age of Migrations. Entire peoples were on the move – not only those Germanic 'nations' that overran most of the Western Roman Empire, but also Slavs and Finno-Ugrians from Eastern

Europe, as well as Huns and other groups from the steppes of south-eastern Europe. Within another century or so several African and Arabian tribal peoples were similarly poised to migrate; in fact, the ancient world all the way from the Roman Mediterranean through Sassanian Iran to India and China was severely disrupted. Practically every cultural or political group, from near-barbaric tribes to sophisticated civilizations, from Ireland to the Chinese frontier and from Siberia to Ethiopia, was involved in wars that would reshape the known world.

Nevertheless, these conflicts did not destroy the ancient Classical cultures, as most of the 'barbarian' conquerors who established new states during these migrations attempted to model their political and, to a lesser degree, their military structures upon those they had overrun. This was clearly the case in the major barbarian kingdoms that dominated a large part of Europe from the late 5th to the 7th century. Meanwhile, the eastern half of the Roman state continued to exist, though in a form that is usually known as the Romano-Byzantine or simply the Byzantine Empire. Elsewhere in the world, several other old empires also survived in a weakened or transformed state, and their armies, like that of Byzantium, both taught and learned from their barbarian rivals.

The last century of the Western Roman Empire had seen military pressure increasing on various fronts, and prompting various responses. Within Central Europe, the Romans tried to maintain control of a strategic corridor lying just north of the Alps. This vital region, providing not only the Empire's easiest east-west overland communications but also an advanced front to protect the Italian heartland, was lost during the early 5th century when the bulk of its defenders were withdrawn to face a Goth invasion of Italy. Meanwhile, in the Eastern Roman Empire, a system of fixed garrisons backed up by field armies continued, until the later 6th century, to work more successfully than it had in the West.

The *Notitia Dignitatum*

Cavalry were clearly vital for such mobile field armies, yet, despite efforts to develop a truly effective cavalry arm, the evidence suggests that Late Roman infantry remained more reliable than Late Roman cavalry. Nevertheless, 54 of the 67 units of archers listed in the *Notitia Dignitatum* – the best surviving source on Late Roman military organization – were mounted. Spear-armed armoured cavalry were not a new idea, but such *cataphracti* also increased in importance during this period; most, though by no means all, were stationed in the Eastern Empire. During the disastrous 5th century, Late Roman armies also evolved a composite spear- and bow-armed armoured cavalryman known as a *hippo-toxotai*. This does seem to have been a new concept for the Romans, and would prove very effective during the 6th-century Romano-Byzantine reconquest of much of the western Mediterranean basin. A smaller élite force of *clibanarii* cavalrymen rode armoured horses, much as did the heavy cavalry of the rival Sassanian Empire of Iran.

The emergence of several different types of specialized troops seems to have been characteristic of the final century of the Western Roman Empire. The *Notitia Dignitatum* lists horse-archers in all parts of the Empire, but most were in the Eastern frontier or garrison forces, while in eastern field armies they were outnumbered by infantry archers. All except one of the

Schematic reconstruction of Hun tactics against a static enemy, showing repeated attacks by horse-archers.

(A) Enemy; (B) Initial positions of horse-archers; (C) Attack positions of horse-archers; (D) Munitions supplies for horse-archers; (E) Armoured support cavalry; (F) Infantry. (After Von Pawlikowski-Cholewa)

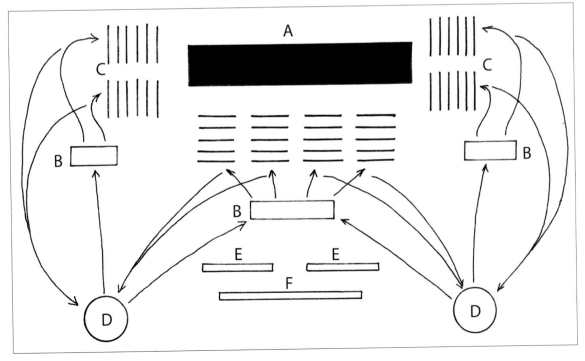

rather obscure *lanciarii* spear-armed infantry units, and *ballistarii* (perhaps troops with crossbow-like weapons mounted in field frames), were also found in an Eastern field army. Specialist river-warfare troops were stationed on the Danube frontier in Central Europe, whereas *dromedarii* camel-mounted infantry were, not surprisingly, listed in Egypt and Palestine. *Exploratores* and *praeventores*, who are believed to have been 'scouts', were mostly based in the West, along with *superventores* (whose nature is vague, but who have been tentatively interpreted as 'rearguard commandos').

Late Roman strategy has inevitably been seen in terms of its failure to save the Western Empire, rather than (as would be more just) of its success in keeping invaders at bay for so long, and for preserving the Eastern Empire almost intact. During the 4th and well into the 5th century, frontier defence came to rely upon a screen of garrisons backed up by mobile field armies. The role of static garrisons was to stop small incursions and to threaten the rear of larger invading forces. If an enemy was denied access to food supplies he was forced to disperse and forage more widely, thus becoming vulnerable to attack by the closest field army, which could then launch reprisal raids into enemy territory. This strategy worked well so long as the crumbling economic power of the Empire could maintain the required forces. Its weakness lay in the fact that field armies were themselves now becoming regionalized and indeed fragmented, because it was only this regional dispersal that enabled such forces to reach raiders before they recrossed the frontier. The Roman army failed to achieve a decisive superiority in cavalry despite great efforts to improve this arm, and similarly, the quality of static frontier troops declined as the Roman economy weakened.

Mosaic panel made between AD 432 and 440, illustrating the Biblical story of Moses and the Amalekites; the soldiers are shown as stylized Late Roman troops. (*in situ* Basilica of Sta Maria Maggiore, Rome)

The aftermath of collapse in the West

Nothing comparable to the *Notitia Dignitatum* exists to shed light on the centuries immediately following the collapse of the Western Roman Empire. Nevertheless, changes can be observed in what might be regarded as typical Mediterranean European strategy and tactics between the fall of the Western Empire in the 5th century and the Muslim-Arab invasions of the early 7th century. These have been described as a shift from a supposedly 'Roman' reliance on iron discipline to a supposedly more 'Greek' emphasis on clever generalship. (While such a potentially racist oversimplification may be dubious, Late Roman or Romano-Byzantine commanders – and those military leaders most strongly influenced by them – certainly demonstrated a growing concern for subtlety, and for misdirecting the enemy by *ruses de guerre*.)

The widespread idea that medieval armies lacked any kind of discipline is clearly outdated and incorrect, and this even seems to have been true of post-Roman, Early Medieval or so-called 'Dark Age' forces. Obviously, Early Medieval military discipline cannot be interpreted in modern terms, any more than strategy and battlefield tactics can be. Commanders simply did the best they could with what they had, in the light of common sense, a will to win, and a desire to minimize their own losses – in other words, they behaved just like any other military leaders down the centuries. Rapid communication systems did not really exist even at the height of the Roman Empire, and battlefield control was rudimentary even in the most sophisticated of pre-modern armies. Consequently, tactics tended to be simple, with certain basic concepts surviving over centuries, if not millennia.

The most obvious variable was the use made of differing terrain, and here the best medieval commanders showed themselves to be as skilful as any in history. This was particularly true when the armies involved were small and consisted largely of one type of troops, either infantry or cavalry. Those commanding larger forces with a greater variety of troop types were able to indulge in more ambitious manoeuvring – sometimes remarkably ambitious, and demonstrating an almost 'modern' grasp of the essentials of geography,

Lightly armoured and unarmoured infantry in combat, in a late 5th-century Roman manuscript. (*Ilias Ambrosiana*, Biblioteca Ambrosiana, Cod. F.205 Inf., Milan)

communications, transport and logistics, as well as the roles of fortifications and of morale.

In tactical rather than strategic terms, the 5th century saw considerable changes. At the start of this period the remaining Roman armies appear to have fought in a rather static manner, leaving most manoeuvres to their 'barbarian' allies or auxiliaries. When fighting the Huns at the battle of Châlons in AD 451, for example, the Late Roman general Flavius Aetius placed his Romans on the traditionally defensive left wing, the reputedly unreliable Alans in the centre (where they were indeed broken by Attila's Huns), and Theodoric and Thorismund's Visigoths on the traditionally offensive right wing (where they were indeed victorious, despite Theodoric's death).

THE AGE OF MIGRATIONS

CAVALRY in the later 5th to 7th centuries

During the 5th century, Roman cavalry formations were still basically the same as those for the infantry, with separate centre and flank divisions, each ideally consisting of a single extended line of horsemen eight ranks deep, without reserves, and relying on one great charge to decide the outcome of a battle. However, this system failed dismally against the Huns and Avars, whose horse-archers could wear it down from a distance, so a new 'ideal' cavalry formation was developed in the Eastern Roman Empire during the late 5th and 6th centuries.

Since cavalry could rarely break disciplined infantry (in this or any other period), the primary role of such Romano-Byzantine armoured cavalry was to menace and render immobile an enemy's footsoldiers, while Romano-Byzantine light cavalry attempted to outflank, harass and even encircle the foe. This involved Romano-Byzantine cavalry operating in smaller but still closely packed units, the resulting *cuneus* formation probably having been copied from steppe peoples. It was then passed on to the Romans' Germanic and Middle Eastern enemies.

By the early 6th century, Romano-Byzantine armies were using sophisticated battlefield manoeuvres involving several different kinds of troops. Like their Sassanian-Persian rivals, the Romano-Byzantines regarded

---

A BATTLE OF CATRAETH, c. AD 600

This represents the failure of an Early Medieval cavalry attack on a Germanic infantry shield-wall. According to *Y Gododdin*, a Welsh poem written not long after the event, the campaign culminated in a confrontation between a force of Romano-Celtic cavalry of the North British kingdom of Gododdin **(A)**, supported by larger numbers of footsoldiers **(B)**, and an infantry force of Northumbrian Angles **(C)**. It would be natural for the Anglo-Saxons to adopt a defensive position, probably on a hill so that their enemies had to attack up a slope. In this 'sub-Roman' period in British history the Romano-Celts would still have been clinging to a Late Roman military tradition, in which javelin-armed cavalry formed the main offensive element. Making repeated attacks, they threw javelins before wheeling aside. Hence they would almost certainly be operating in formations, though these would probably be ragged. The Anglo-Saxons might also be imitating Late Roman tactics in a rudimentary manner, probably as an elongated mass of infantry, with the few armoured men standing at the front, and few, if any, horsemen.

Inset 1: The ranks of a shield-wall, rather formalized here to make distinctions between different levels of equipment. We show the front rank armoured and armed with shield and sword; the second rank men with shields supported on a guige, so that they can hold a spear with both hands; and a third rank throwing javelins over the heads of the first two.

Inset 2: Aristocratic armoured Romano-Celtic cavalrymen were armed with javelins and spears. These two horsemen ride without stirrups. One throws a javelin – his legs have to grip tightly in order to provide a stable platform; the second uses both hands to thrust with a spear, which makes carrying a shield difficult, if not impossible.

Part of an iron lamellar armour found in Hungary. It is either Late Roman, or from a people of recent steppe origin. (Budapest Historical Museum, Budapest; author's photograph)

cavalry as a military élite. By the early 7th century, the Byzantines had trained their best men to use bows on horseback, only those unable to do this being trained with spear and shield. The new 'ideal' cavalry formation now consisted of two lines of horsemen about 400 yards/metres apart, the rear line consisting of one third of the total and acting as a reserve. Both lines were also trained to change front if threatened from the rear. There were more armoured men at the front, flanks and rear, and those at the front included men on armoured horses. This protected the animal against arrows so that the rider could resist harassment by horse-archers, and get close enough to his foe to use close-combat weapons. Each division consisted of offensive *cursores* armed with bows, who were protected by similarly armed *defensores*. The latter followed their *cursores'* repeated attacks closely, though there were more *cursores* on the wings and more *defensores* in the centre.

Romano-Byzantine armies clearly used the traditional nomadic tactic of feigned flight, even being trained to drop non-essential items of equipment to make such flights more convincing. The ambush was an even more favoured tactic. One feature that stands out as almost universally characteristic of battle from the mid 7th to mid 8th century was the attempt by both sides to storm an enemy's encampment, which was placed at a greater or lesser distance behind his battle-line.

The various cavalry tactics descibed in the *Strategikon* attributed to the Emperor Maurice (r. AD 582–602) were clearly used in battle. The feigned flight was, for example, known as the 'Scythian ambush', whereas in training the 'Scythian drill' was basically an encircling movement. The 'Alan drill' consisted of a single line of attackers and defenders making repeated attacks and withdrawals. While the 'African drill' specified a single line with defenders in the middle and attackers on both flanks, the 'Italian drill' was considered the best, consisting of two mixed lines of attackers and defenders.

The steppe peoples

The fact that two of these drills plus the ambush were named after the Romano-Byzantines' steppe neighbours highlights the military signifiance of these peoples. However, even before the various waves of nomad conquerors or refugees left the Eurasian steppes to enter a largely forested and agricultural Europe, their armies included several different types of troops.

The Alans, for example, were described as having many well-armoured cavalrymen fighting with bow and spear, though they also had infantrymen to protect their few vital remaining horse pastures. The fearsome Huns are sometimes said to have 'dismounted' on entering Central Europe in the 4th century – they were, in fact, mostly described as fighting on foot during the 5th century, and as using large shields of obvious infantry form. Meanwhile many of these Hunnish infantry remained very effective archers. Overall it is clear that the later Huns in Central Europe fought in a very different manner from the earlier Huns north of the Black Sea; indeed, there were almost no references to Hun cavalry or fast-raiding nomadic Hun horsemen after the Hunnish people entered the Balkans in the late 4th century. By the 5th century the Huns appeared more like raiders than conquerors; they could be ambushed by almost static Roman forces, and tended to get defeated whenever they faced regular Roman troops in battle. Similarly, it is noteworthy that many of the major Hun raids were carried out at a time of year when there was very little grass available for their supposedly large numbers of horses. In addition, Hun raids were often described as being slowed down by large wagons in which they carried their booty.

The battlefield tactics of other nomadic Early Medieval steppe forces and their descendants within Europe are less well documented than those of later centuries. The Alans, for example, were described as fighting in highly manoeuvrable, close-packed units, armed with javelins and swords, and employing feigned retreats and flank attacks. Unlike the Huns, the 6th-century

Avars seem to have retained a greater element of cavalry after settling in Central Europe. Nevertheless, the Avar and allied Slav army that besieged Constantinople in AD 626 included many armoured footsoldiers, some of whom are believed to have come from the dominant Avar élite that also provided the armoured horsemen. The sophisticated Avars, whose civil and military culture both betray strong Chinese influence, were described as fighting in close-packed cavalry formations. The more primitive Slavs, by contrast, seem to have relied on ambush tactics in close country, using javelins, poisoned arrows and large infantry shields, followed up by a sudden massed infantry charge.

Germanic armies

Not surprisingly, Germanic armies, even those of the most successful 'successor' states, did not include such a sophisticated array of troop types as did Late Roman or Romano-Byzantine armies. The Anglo-Saxons in Britain apparently fought only on foot. The Ostrogoths, Visigoths and several other Germanic peoples had infantry archers, but did not generally use the powerful composite bows typical of both steppe peoples and Romano-Byzantine armies. The Vandals, Alemanni and Visigoths included larger numbers of horsemen than other Germanic forces, and much of the fighting between Visigoths and Franks in southern Gaul was carried out by mounted troops. In the Iberian peninsula, cavalry traditions appear to have survived more vigorously than elsewhere in ex-Roman Western Europe. It has even been suggested that the Visigothic period in Spain and Portugal saw a mixing of Romano-Celtic and Germanic Visigoth cavalry traditions to produce something new, which may then have contributed to the emergence of distinctive Christian and Muslim Iberian styles of cavalry warfare during the medieval period. Furthermore, there is tantalizing evidence to suggest that later 6th- and 7th-century Visigothic armies even included some horse-archers – perhaps a tactic learned from the Byzantine-ruled regions of southern Andalusia.

Battle of Taginae, AD 552, in which a Romano-Byzantine army under Narses, with Germanic Lombard and Herul allies, defeated the Ostrogoths under King Totila.

Initial dispositions: (A) Roman cavalry; (B) Roman archers; (C) Lombards & Heruli; (D) Roman infantry in defensive position on hill; (E) Ostrogoth cavalry; (F) Ostrogoth infantry.

Movements: (1) Ostrogoth flanking movement is defeated; (2) Sudden Ostrogoth cavalry assault attempts to catch Narses' German allies 'at lunch'; (3) Romano-Byzantine archers swing forward to shoot at Ostrogoth flanks, forcing them to fall back. The entire Ostrogoth army then fled.

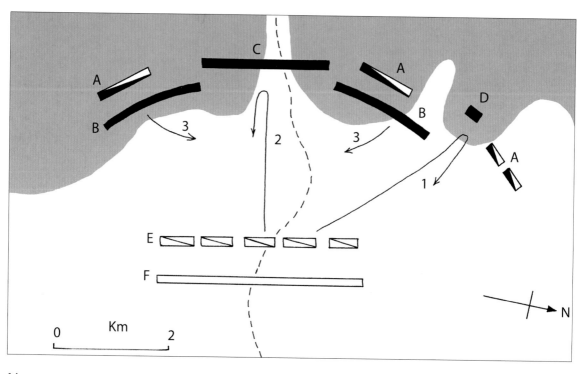

Similarly, there are plenty of references to Frankish cavalry in the 5th century, though by the middle of the 6th the Frankish invasions of Italy appear to have been largely infantry affairs. While there seem to be fewer references to Frankish horsemen in the later Merovingian period than in the earlier decades, the Lombards who invaded Italy in the 6th century did make greater use of cavalry than previous Germanic invaders. Altogether there seems to have been considerable variety within Germanic armies, and the traditional view that this was a period during which Europe saw a revival in the importance of infantry and a decline in that of cavalry seems to be an oversimplification.

The strategic thinking of Germanic leaders at the time of the Great Migrations is largely unknown, but the way in which rulers of their successor kingdoms dealt with varied military problems indicates that they were capable of broad strategic planning. Frankish forces, for example, were noted for a high degree of mobility, and it was this that enabled their Merovingian kings to vary their strategy according to circumstances. Merovingian warfare within the kingdom, or during campaigns intended to extend its frontiers, was primarily aimed at the taking and keeping of cities and fortified *castrae*. Punitive or predatory warfare beyond the kingdom largely consisted of raiding for booty and extracting tribute from neighbouring peoples. Much the same was true of other Germanic states, though the Visigoths of the Iberian peninsula did face a specific problem in the form of almost continually rebellious Basques in the north of the country.

The invading Germanic peoples were equally varied in the sophistication or otherwise of their battlefield tactics. One such was the early Germanic tactic of combined cavalry and light infantry assaults, which had been used against the Romans centuries before. This tactic was based on a family or tribal formation described by their Roman opponents as resembling a *cuneus* or 'wedge'. It was tactically similar to the harassment techniques of the steppe peoples, though the latter relied overwhelmingly on mounted troops.

Other aspects of Germanic tactics during the Age of Migrations suggest Sassanian influence from Iran, again transmitted via the nomadic peoples who invaded Eastern and Central Europe. The Visigoths, for example, clearly used the typically Eastern tactic of the feigned retreat, perhaps having learned it during their long migrations across Eastern Europe. Once settled within the Iberian peninsula, however, Visigothic cavalry seem to have relied largely on tactics of repeated attack and withdrawal, almost certainly learned from their Late Roman or Romano-Byzantine foes. In Italy, Ostrogothic infantry archers fought under the protection of their own cavalry, again reflecting Romano-Byzantine practice. It is also interesting to note that, according to a 6th-century

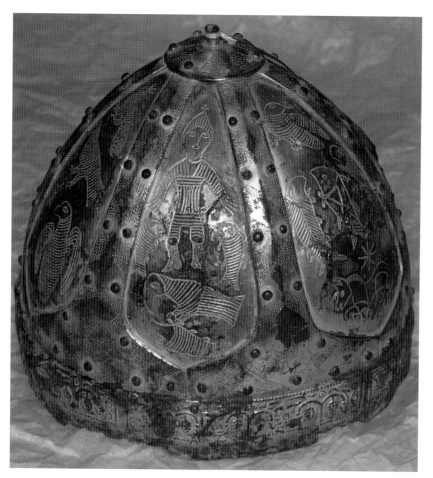

Gilded bronze and iron *spangenhelm* from southern Russia, 6th or 7th century. The decorated rim shows that it was of Byzantine origin, while the crude Christian symbols on the segments suggests that it was used by a newly Christianized barbarian people. (Private collection; author's photograph)

military manual, Romano-Byzantine troops should beware of an enemy (probably meaning the Ostrogoths in Italy) disguising themselves in Roman equipment so that they could get close to the Romans without being identified.

During a relatively well-recorded battle in AD 507, the Franks drew up their archers and javelin-throwers behind other presumably spear-armed infantry when facing the Visigoths; Frankish cavalry were also present, but served in an unspecified role. There appear to have been few changes in Frankish tactics during the Merovingian period, the available cavalry being used largely for raiding and the pursuit of an already beaten foe, with no clear evidence of cavalry charges during a battle. On the other hand, in AD 531 Thuringian Germans attempted to catch Frankish horsemen in ditch-traps, recalling a tactic used by Hephthalite White Huns against the Sassanian Persians during the previous century. During the 6th century, Burgundian troops (in reality perhaps Romano-Burgundians) trapped a force of Lombard cavalry in a forested, mountainous area by blocking the road with felled trees. Elsewhere it is clear that both Frankish and Lombardic horsemen would dismount to fight on foot if they got into difficulties.

Post-Roman Britain

Even less information survives concerning the Romano-British and Celtic armies of post-Roman Britain and across the English Channel in Brittany. Surviving Romano-Celtic urban militias would have been almost entirely infantry, but outside the shrinking cities there may have been greater variation. The tribal peoples of Wales and south-western Britain would again have been mostly footsoldiers, while there may have been greater numbers of horsemen in the Pennines and West Midlands. The great majority, if not all of such horsemen would nevertheless have ridden relatively small Celtic horses or large ponies, since there is as yet no evidence that larger horses were bred within northern and western Britain. The horsemen would seem to have been armed with javelins and spears, operating in the style of earlier Roman skirmishing cavalry rather than Late Roman *cataphracti*.

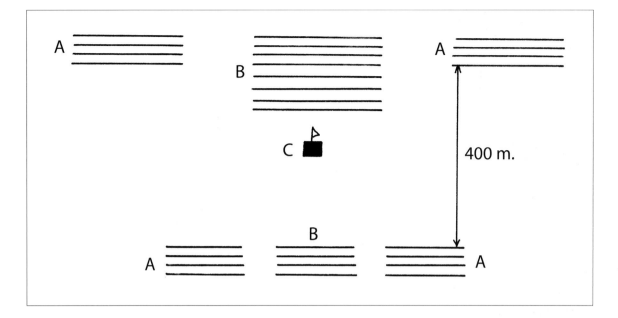

It is generally assumed that there was no broad strategy in 5th to 7th century Britain, and that warfare was merely an 'aristocratic way of life'. It is probably true that, for the Romano-Celtic British, warfare was based upon guerrilla-style raids, intended to halt or evict creeping Anglo-Saxon colonization. On the other hand, the few surviving sources suggest a distinction between the short-range campaigns of the 6th century and the sometimes much longer-range campaigns of the 7th century. *Y Gododdin*, a Welsh North British poem of the 7th century, almost certainly recalled an ambitious though unsuccessful Romano-Celtic attempt to split the Anglo-Saxon region of Bernicia (Northumberland) from that of Deira (Yorkshire), in what would have been a clear case of broad strategic thinking.

The very inadequate written evidence might indicate a tactical preference for sudden dawn attacks on the part of Romano-British forces, perhaps after long night marches. Even the epic *Y Gododdin*, which is the best surviving source, only partially clarifies the tactical role of cavalry in battle. Some may have been mounted infantry who actually fought on foot, others merely the leaders of otherwise infantry troops. Those who remained on horseback appear to have fought with javelins, spears and swords, while their *pedyt* or footsoldiers drew up in ranks, or in a phalanx described as a 'battle square' or 'like a cattle pen'. The overall Romano-Celtic *dull* or battle array was supposed to have had a vanguard, centre and wings, with the men fighting in close formation, each unit under a recognized leader.

Fighting on horseback

Late Roman, early Romano-Byzantine and other Early Medieval cavalry in Western Europe had not yet adopted stirrups, but this did not limit the effectiveness of a horseman to anything like the extent that is popularly believed. This was particularly true after the wood-framed saddle had been adopted, since this provided its rider with plenty of support. Most early Roman cavalry had been armed with javelins rather than thrusting spears, but longer spears were widely adopted under Sarmatian and Alan influence during the 4th century. At this time there were four basic ways of using

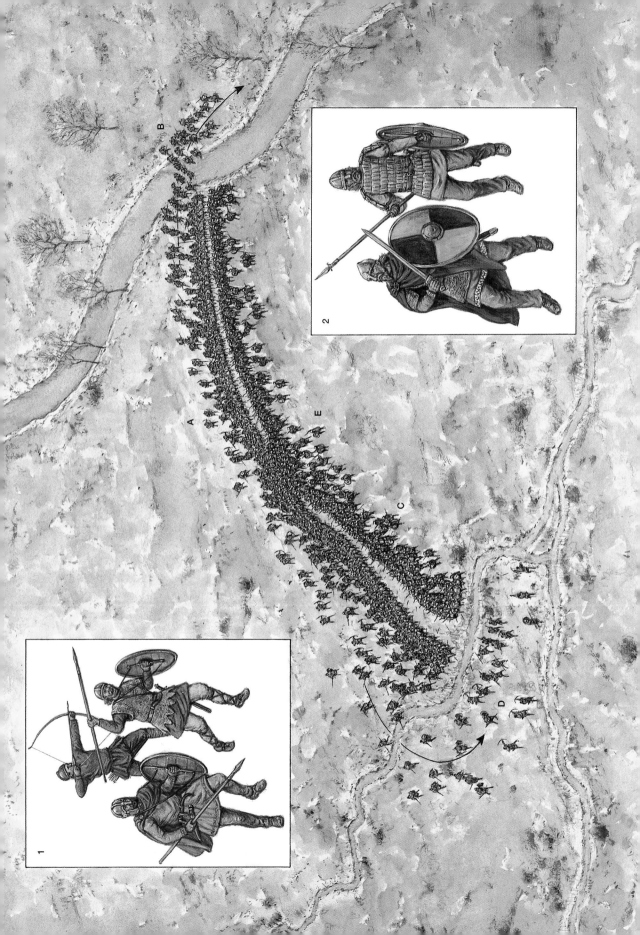

a spear on horseback: throwing it as a javelin, thrusting downwards with a raised arm, thrusting forwards by swinging the arm, or thrusting with a two-handed grip.

During this period the two-handed method of thrusting with a cavalry spear predominated and was clearly effective, even against an armoured foe. The weapon was, nevertheless, normally pointed along the right side of the horse's head, not to the left as was normal with the *couched* lance when horsemen were *jousting* against each other. Both two-handed and single-handed thrusting techniques enabled a cavalryman to retrieve his weapon with relative ease; this would not be the case with the couched lance, since this latter style was essentially a once-only shock technique.

Unlike later knights with their couched lances, earlier spear-armed cavalrymen rarely used shields, these still generally being associated with close-quarter weapons such as the sword. Occasional references to small shields being strapped to a spearman's upper arm to protect his neck and face may, however, indicate that such shields had widely spaced inner straps of the kind later called *enarmes*; here the man thrust his left arm right through such straps and out beyond them, rather than gripping one in his fist.

Unlike the Sassanian Persians, Romano-Byzantine archers both on foot and horseback appear to have placed the emphasis on the power and accuracy rather than the speed of shooting. Both Romano-Byzantine and Sassanian horse-archery was usually employed while the mount was standing still. Romano-Byzantine archers were advised to vary their 'draw' or technique of pulling back the bowstring, using various styles of finger-draw as well as the more powerful thumb-draw. They were also trained to shoot at a lateral angle into the enemies' ranks, in the hope of getting arrows around the edges of their shields.

Quite why the Roman and Iranian 'four-horned' saddle was abandoned in the late 4th and the 5th century remains a mystery, since experiments have shown that it provided excellent support for a rider wielding a sword or spear. However, the Emperor Constantine reportedly introduced a new saddle to 'strengthen the solidity of the rider's seat', while the precise weight of such saddles was enshrined in the Emperor Theodosius II's legal code of AD 438.

B 'SHIELD-WALL/SHIELD-FORT' TACTICS, c. AD 850

An archetypal confrontation between an Anglo-Saxon *fyrd* of local troops and part-time warriors, and a Viking raiding force, to demonstrate variations on a basic 'shield-wall' versus 'shield-fort' clash between unequal forces that include no cavalry.

On this occasion the Anglo-Saxons **(A)** are the more numerous but less well-equipped force; they have concentrated their few armoured men in the centre. They use their numerical advantage to try to outflank the Vikings, or force them to extend their line until it is weakened enough to be broken. At **(B)**, skirmishers, javelin-throwers and a much smaller number of archers are making their way across the tidal stream upon which the Vikings **(C)** have anchored their 'unshielded' right flank. The Vikings are not numerous enough to extend their left flank to another similarly strong obstacle, but curl the left end of their line backwards in the beginnings of a rudimentary 'shield-fort'. The Anglo-Saxons have thinned out their centre to send forward on this flank, too, a few archers **(D)**, who shoot at the raiders' flank from a safe distance. By contrast, the Vikings are using their advantage in weight and perhaps quality of equipment by strengthening one point in their line **(E)**, in an attempt to break the Anglo-Saxon line.

This is no longer the 'sub-Roman' period, and there is no evidence that Northern European armies attempted to make regularly shaped formations. Nevertheless, the front ranks in both forces are an élite of strong, well-armoured young men.

Inset 1: Three typical Anglo-Saxon warriors. At left is a moderately well-equipped *fyrd* man, at right a more lightly equipped javelin-thrower, and behind them an unarmoured archer.

Inset 2: The best-equipped of Scandinavian Viking raiders reflected an ideal of Northern European infantry warfare in terms of arms, armour and ferocity, and were soon in demand as mercenaries far and wide.

Perhaps the nomad form of framed saddle, as used by Huns, Avars and other subsequent waves of invaders, was more suitable for a horse-archer.

Nor did all peoples immediately adopt the stirrup, which is widely seen as one of the most significant technological developments of the early Middle Ages. Stirrups were used throughout the Eurasian steppes before the start of the 7th century; Romano-Byzantine cavalry probably adopted them by the end of the 6th century, and the earliest Byzantine documentary reference to them is in the *Strategikon*. The Byzantines may, in fact, have adopted stirrups before the notably cavalry-orientated Sassanian Persians.

INFANTRY in the later 5th to 9th centuries

The abundance of surviving written evidence dealing with the Romano-Byzantine armies of this period indicates the very precise training involved in the setting-up and defence of encampments and field fortifications. In the 6th century this went so far as to ensure that, while inside their tents, men kept their spears upright at their feet with their shield resting on the spearshaft and having its holding-straps towards the man, while the rest of a sleeping

A Romano-Byzantine wood carving from Ashmunein in Egypt, 6th or 7th century, showing armoured cavalry and infantry. (Berlin; carving destroyed during World War II)

man's kit was all arranged at his left side. Beyond the camp's perimeter, spiked *calthrops* were scattered – not necessarily to cause serious injuries, but to lame an enemy's horse, and hopefully make either the animal or its owner cry out and thus alert a sentry.

Many armies, including the Byzantine, often travelled with their families as well as substantial supply and siege trains, and thus needed large, well-protected camps. Once again the *Strategikon* supplies interesting details, including reference to numerous *paraportia* or small 'gates' in such field fortifications, probably for cavalry sorties. Another new development for the Byzantines was the use of carts as a form of field defence – an early form of *wagenburg*, which had almost certainly been copied from steppe foes such as the Huns or Avars. These carts appear to have formed an outer defence guarded by infantry archers, with a wide *intervallum* between them and the heavy infantry, while cavalry were stationed at the centre of the camp.

The sources suggest that there were also changes in Romano-Byzantine infantry battlefield formations, though these seem to have been relatively minor compared to changes in cavalry formations. For example, 6th-century formations were still described as being square or rectangular, each file commanded by an officer, with the *ilarch* or unit leader in the front rank.

Nevertheless, the emphasis placed upon an infantry formation's ability to change front rapidly may have been new. If enemy cavalry attacked only from the front, these infantry formations would be preceded by unarmoured skirmishers armed with slings. The front two ranks of the main formation would shoot their bows horizontally against the enemy's horses, those to the rear shooting high to drop their arrows on the enemy, thus hopefully forcing them to raise their shields and thus expose their horses to arrows. The infantrymen would place their spears on the ground and only pick them up if the enemy came close. An emphasis on the need to be able to wheel a formation about and change its shape reveals a concern about the dangers of surprise attack. References to Byzantine infantry being chained together to stop them retreating were, like later such stories, a poetical misunderstanding or exaggeration of the 'shield-wall' tactics in which soldiers stood side by side in close order, each attempting to defend both himself and those behind him and, in the most disciplined armies, those on either side.

Most peoples of originally nomadic steppe origin made considerable use of large wagons for transport, though more rarely in battle. Once inside Europe, however, the Alans were described as drawing such wagons into a defensive circle at night. For their part, the now largely dismounted Turco-Mongol Huns of Attila's army established a hilltop field fortification of wagons at the battle of Châlons, to which they retreated when bested by the Romans and Visigoths. This would not normally be considered a steppe nomad tactic – though it is true that the Mongol armies of the later Middle Ages did use wagon encampments.

Even less is known about field fortification in Germanic armies, though the Merovingians clearly did use some kind of wooden defences against

An iron curb-bit from southern Spain, dating from the 7th or early 8th century; note the massive *psalions* or cheek-pieces. (inv. 1947.1000.24, Metropolitan Museum of Art, New York; author's photograph)

21

mounted foes during a civil war early in the 6th century. The tactical sophistication of invading Germanic peoples was clearly very varied. At one extreme, the 5th- and early 6th-century Anglo-Saxons hardly seem to have had tactics at all in any meaningful sense. They may have fought as effective guerrilla raiders in forested areas, but there is no evidence of Anglo-Saxon warriors combining cavalry and light infantry assaults, as had been used against the Romans long before.

Of course, nothing comparable to Romano-Byzantine training manuals exist for 'barbarian' Western Europe, so any understanding of how Germanic warriors fought must rely on highly coloured epic myths and on archaeological evidence which is difficult to interpret. Earlier Roman sources indicated that the Germans used lighter parrying shields than the Romans' own heavy *scutum*, and a subsequent development of this tradition is borne out by excavated Anglo-Saxon shield bosses. From the 5th century onwards more substantial shield bosses appeared, though still on light shields, and their shape suggests an effort to parry or trap an enemy's sword-blade. During the 6th century thicker, heavier and perhaps larger shields came into use, their bosses again being relatively thin but more pronounced; these suggest an effort to deflect blows from straight ahead, and imply a more passive use of the shield. This shape continued to develop throughout the 7th century, becoming larger, thicker and stronger. The nature of battle-damage suffered by surviving shield bosses suggests an individual duelling type of warfare in the earliest phase, without much use of javelins or other missile weapons. Subsequently, the men owning later types of shield bosses appear to have fought in more disciplined ranks or in mutually supportive formations, holding their shields more steadily, and apparently now concerned only with threats from their immediate front. Elsewhere in Europe particular peoples had their own combat styles, the 6th-century Franks' use of characteristic *franciska* throwing-axes being merely the most distinctive.

The little evidence that survives concerning Romano-British warfare suggests a reliance on small, highly mobile mounted forces, and in such circumstances field fortifications are unlikely to have been used. If they did exist, they would presumably have been a more limited continuation of Late Roman forms. In Romano-Celtic Britain assaults on strongholds or prepared positions were

BATTLE OF THE LECH, AD 955

This battle was won because the well-armoured German cavalry on the right wing of Emperor Otto the Great's army were able to make a sudden assault, which caught the horse-archers on the left wing of the Magyar-Hungarian army by surprise.

Infantry formed the centres of both armies, in each case flanked by cavalry; both the Ottonian (A) and the Magyar and subordinate infantry (B) have their best-armoured men in the centre and on the flanks. Previous manoeuvring by the German army had probably managed to over-extend the Magyar horse-archers, who deployed in dispersed groups of 20–50 men (C). When the German cavalry charged suddenly, in close-packed formations of about 20 men each (D), they hit the Magyar horse-archers before the latter could loose more than one or two volleys of arrows, thus reducing German casualties. This, and the previous over-extension of the Hungarian left-wing cavalry, enabled the German cavalry to swing left behind the Hungarian infantry once the horse-archers had been forced back. The battle concluded when the bulk of the Magyar horse-archers on both flanks fled, leaving their infantry to be caught between the Ottonian cavalry and infantry. A final attempt by the Magyar cavalry to lure the Germans into pursuing them, to give the Hungarian infantry a chance to escape, failed.

Inset 1: Part of a close-packed Western European *cuneus* cavalry formation, which differs from the later medieval *conrois* in that it did not rely only on the couched lance. Here the riders hold their large shields high as a protection against arrows, while wielding their spears overarm.

Inset 2: Magyar horse-archers using their bows in the Sassanian-Byzantine manner, 'shower-shooting' in ranks that were usually static, rather than – as in the Turco-Mongol method – while dispersed and on the move.

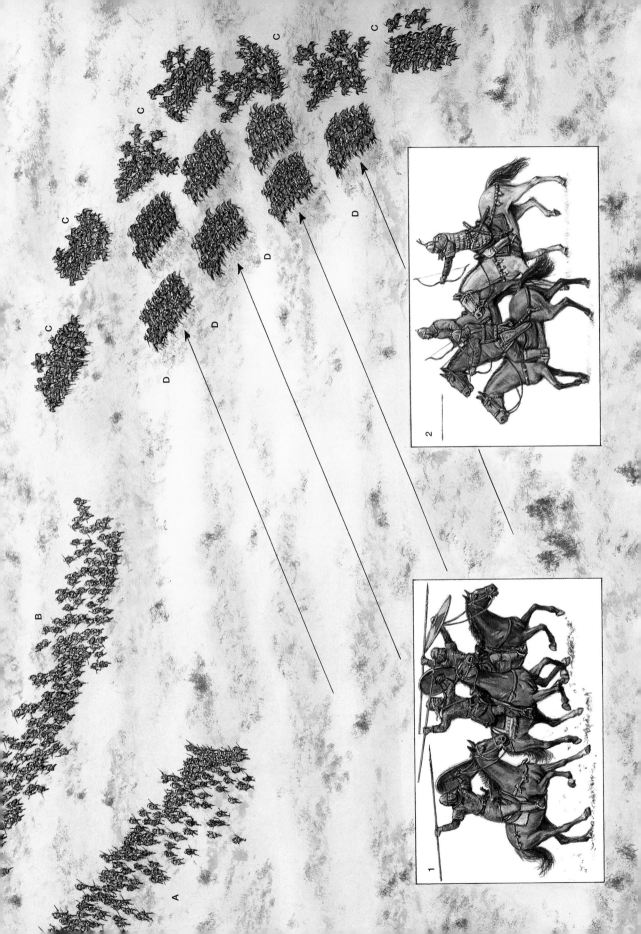

A

B

C

C

C

C

C

C

C

D

D

D

D

D

1

2

rare, though there were sieges – or at least, battles outside fortified places. The purpose of the long dykes and ditches which were constructed during this period remains mysterious. It would be impractical for them to serve as extended fortifications, but the narrow gaps in them perhaps served as choke-points where enemy raiders returning home with rustled cattle or other plunder might be attacked. (Perhaps we should also recall the earlier Roman use of the regular gates in the Hadrian's Wall system for sorties.)

Of all forms of personal protection the shield was the most widespread. The limited archaeological evidence indicates that Romano-Celtic Britain and Celtic Ireland continued a Roman tradition of using relatively thin shields with small bosses, whereas the shields of the Anglo-Saxons and other Germanic peoples were generally larger. *Y Gododdin* describes the white, lime-washed shields of its heroes – a motif also found in the earliest written Irish sources. The supposed 'punching' pointed bosses found in early Anglo-Saxon burials also bring to mind a passage in a 6th-century Romano-Byzantine manual, which refers to the shields of the front rank of an infantry formation having spiked thrusting-bosses.

The question of Early Medieval hand-held (as distinct from frame-mounted) crossbows remains to be resolved. These had been used by Chinese infantry since at least the 4th century BC. Small hunting crossbows are shown on Roman carvings from Gaul, but these are very different from those of China, perhaps having revolving string-release nuts like those of medieval European and Middle Eastern crossbows. Such revolving crossbow-nuts have been found in a presumed Roman or perhaps Romano-Celtic grave in western England, and in a 6th- or 7th-century site in south-western Scotland; a crossbow is also clearly shown in a Pictish carving, again from Early Medieval Scotland. What can be said with reasonable certainty is that the hand-held crossbow never quite died out in Western Europe, probably surviving as a hunting weapon until its revival in a military context in various parts of southern Europe during the 10th or 11th century.

EARLY MEDIEVAL CAVALRY & INFANTRY

The 7th to early 10th centuries

The idea that an Arab and Berber Islamic threat from the south prompted a sudden conversion to cavalry warfare within Carolingian armies during the 8th century has now been disproved, not least because the western Islamic armies of this period still consisted largely of infantry or mounted infantry rather than large numbers of true cavalry. If any external threat did prompt the rise of cavalry in mainland Western Europe, it was that posed by Magyars, by Vikings and later Islamic seaborne raiders in the 9th and 10th centuries. Nevertheless, the later Carolingians' relative lack of strategic mobility may have led to their reliance on initially static tactics against Viking raiders.

The most dramatic development in horse harness during these centuries was the adoption of stirrups. As mentioned above, many historians have over-emphasized the significance of the stirrup as an aid to the effective use of weapons. What is not so widely recognized is the fact that stirrups also gave support to the rider's legs during long-distance rides, and reduced the effects of cold by improving the circulation in his legs. It is probably significant that

A bronze aquamanile in the form of a horse with the new type of framed saddle; Byzantine, 8th–9th century. (Hermitage Museum, St Petersburg; author's photograph)

stirrups were developed in one of the coldest horse-rearing regions of the world, where more or less nomadic peoples spent a large part of their lives in the saddle.

All-rope or leather 'toe stirrups' had been known in India since the 1st century AD, and continued to be used in Africa and elsewhere until modern times. The fully developed rigid stirrup was invented in eastern Asia,

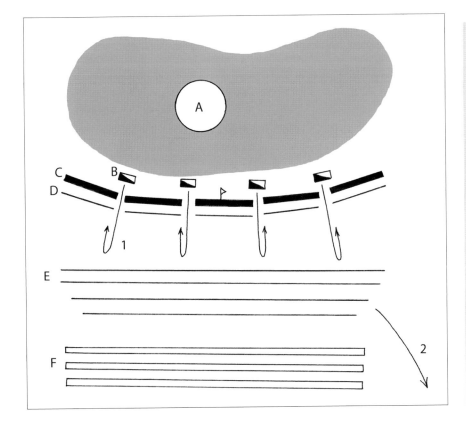

Battle of Guadalete, July AD 711, in which a small Umayyad army of Muslim Arabs and Berbers routed the army of Visigothic Iberia under King Roderic. The little that is known about this epoch-making confrontation indicates that the Muslim invaders had very few cavalry, though these were probably used in a manner typical of Umayyad armies in the Caliphate's Middle Eastern heartlands.

Initial dispositions: (**A**) Muslim camp, almost certainly on raised ground; (**B**) Muslim cavalry; (**C**) Muslim infantry spearmen; (**D**) Muslim infantry archers; (**E**) Visigoth cavalry; (**F**) Visigoth infantry.

Movements: (**1**) Selective attacks by Muslim cavalry, presumably against advancing Visigoths; (**2**) The desertion by Sisibert with the Visigoths' right wing is perhaps only legendary, though an element of the army probably did 'stand aside'.

either in the eastern steppe regions or in Korea or northern China. Rigid stirrups are first mentioned in written sources in 5th-century China, where the first illustration was also found, dating from a century later. The earliest known example comes from 4th-century north-eastern China, and has a wooden step. Wholly or partially wooden stirrups continued to be used in Central Asia, the Caucasus and Russia for many centuries, though few survive.

Stirrups were clearly used by the Juan-Juan nomads of China's northern frontier in the 5th century, and the Avar descendants of these people brought cast bronze or iron stirrups to Europe. The Avars are then generally credited with a sudden spread of rigid stirrups in the West, the Romano-Byzantines having adopted them by the end of the 6th century. However, Islamic sources state that neither stirrups nor the associated wood-framed saddle were being used by Andalusian cavalry even by the 10th century, while a hundred years later Arab Andalusian and Christian Iberian documents indicate that two quite different forms of saddle were still in use, the Arab-Andalusian and the Berber (though quite which one of these was the padded type with a high pommel and low cantle is unclear).

Another important development was the reintroduction of horseshoes – probably via the Muslims, whose cavalry technology reflected the stony terrain of their Middle Eastern homelands. A new form of more supportive wood-framed saddle may also have reflected Middle Eastern Islamic and Byzantine inspiration, though steppe influence also played a part. This new saddle was associated with breast and crupper straps around the front and rear of the horse, and, for several centuries, with doubled girths beneath the animal's body. All were designed,

The battle scene carved on the back of the 8th-century cross-slab at Aberlemno in Scotland. The horsemen are mostly armed with javelins and shields. The array of footsoldiers has swordsmen at the front, supported by spearmen behind; note also their sharply protruding shield bosses. (*in situ* Churchyard, Aberlemno; author's photographs)

at least in part, to keep the saddle in place during the stresses of mounted combat. The breast-strap in particular may have been even more important to the development of combat with the couched lance than was the deep saddle, or indeed stirrups. The raised pommel and cantle of the deep or 'peaked' saddle gave the rider with a couched lance greater support when he, his weapon and his horse came in contact with their target, and the widespread adoption of the breast-strap in the 11th century may have been either a contributory factor to, or a consequence of, the adoption of the couched lance.

Contrary to widespread belief, horse-armour became more rather than less widespread in the early Middle Ages, at least among the Byzantines and their Muslim neighbours, while it remained unknown in Western Europe apart from the Muslim-ruled region of Iberia. In the 8th century, Byzantine horse-armour may still have been in the Avar style, covering only the front of the animal; however, by the 10th century some horse-armours or *bards* – made of layers of glued felt, of iron or hardened leather *lamellae* – covered the entire animal from head to tail, and hung down almost to its feet. There are even possible references to mail horse-armour in the 11th century. Felt horse-armour (known in Islamic regions as *tijfaf*) was used in late 10th-century Andalusia. Most remarkable of all are several references to items of 10th- and 11th-century Andalusian and Christian Iberian armour known variously as *tashtina*, *testinia* and *tishtani*. These could be 'plated' or gilded, and were probably very early versions of the *chamfron*, the rigid head-protection for a horse that was generally known in 13th- and 14th-century Europe by the French term *testière*.

This allegorical figure of 'War', dating from AD 790–800, provides the earliest realistic representation of a fully armoured Carolingian cavalryman. (*Gellone Sacramentary*, Bib. Nationale, Ms. Lat. 12048, Paris)

Motivation and tactics

Most military commanders of this period may have tried to avoid full-scale battles, but when these were fought the primary aim was normally to kill or capture the enemy commander, since an Early Medieval army – like its ancient predecessors – would almost inevitably collapse if this was achieved. As a result, during this period European strategy was almost entirely based upon raiding and ravaging, to inflict as much physical and economic damage as possible. While this reflected a famous statement by the late Roman theoretician Vegetius, that 'famine is more terrible than the sword', it is highly unlikely that more than a tiny handful of Early Medieval commanders had ever heard of Vegetius.

The common soldier fought either in the hope of profit, frequently in the form of portable loot, or, conversely, in defence of his home and family and to limit the damage caused by enemy ravaging. In more sophisticated armies this involved attacking a raiding force's supply lines and harassing its foragers, but only engaging it in open battle as a last resort or if the conditions were unusually favourable. The main problem facing both attackers and

The Carolingian *Psalterium Auraeum* manuscript contains several battle scenes, including this picture of cavalry and infantry attacking a fortified place. (Library, Cod. 22, p.141, Monastery of St Gall, Switzerland)

defenders remained that of maintaining their armies in the field for as long as possible, in a period when, and in areas where, logistical support and the ability to feed or pay troops was at best rudimentary.

The evolution of the couched-lance style of cavalry combat in Western Europe during the 9th to 11th centuries was highly significant, although in fact it would eventually prove to be a tactical dead-end. This technique was not, however, a Western European invention, as is still widely believed, but was copied from Europe's Byzantine and Islamic neighbours. With a 'couched' lance the weapon was held tightly beneath a rider's upper arm, using the forward momentum of his horse to give impetus to its strike. All of the other three cavalry spear techniques already mentioned (see above, 'Fighting on horseback') continued to be used alongside the couched lance in Byzantine and many Islamic forces; they also survived in Western Europe well into – and in many places throughout – the 11th century.

Small tactical formations of densely packed armoured cavalry, suited to the couched-lance technique, existed during Carolingian times, despite the fact that such formations had originally been designed for repeated attack-and-withdrawal tactics inherited from the Late Roman Empire. The Carolingian *cuneus* or *conrois* formations, like the *acie* or *liek* of 10th-century Germany, seem normally to have comprised about 50 men.

Meanwhile, Byzantine sources indicate that 10th-century Bulgarian armies fought in ordered ranks rather than using archetypal nomadic dispersal or harassment tactics. Perhaps this was because Bulgarian armies now included many Slav warriors, or because the Bulgars were culturally and perhaps

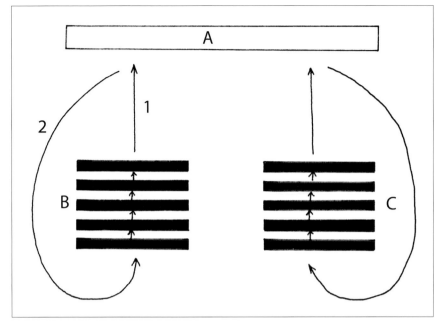

ethnically descended from those Huns who had returned to the western steppes after the collapse of Attila's empire back in the 5th century. The Slavs themselves were described as having virtually no 'order of battle'; they relied on a single noisy charge, and if this failed they supposedly abandoned the fight.

The little that is known of Christian Iberian battlefield tactics at this time indicates that cavalry still used the *turna-fuye* tactic of repeated charges and withdrawals, as used by Late Roman horsemen and continued by Muslim Arab cavalry (who knew it as *karr wa farr*). A detailed study of the many *Mozarab* or 'Arabized' Christian manuscripts from the Iberian peninsula suggests that spears were sometimes thrown as javelins, sometimes used for both thrusting and lateral cuts, and sometimes had blades at both ends. They could be used with both hands when not carrying a shield, but only with one hand if a shield was being used. Duels between opposing champions before the start of a battle were common among both Muslims and Christians in the Iberian peninsula, sometimes culminating in a brutal wrestling match on horseback or on the ground.

Battlefield tactics in Anglo-Saxon England and in Scandinavia remained simpler, apparently nearly always being characterized by a solid array of men on

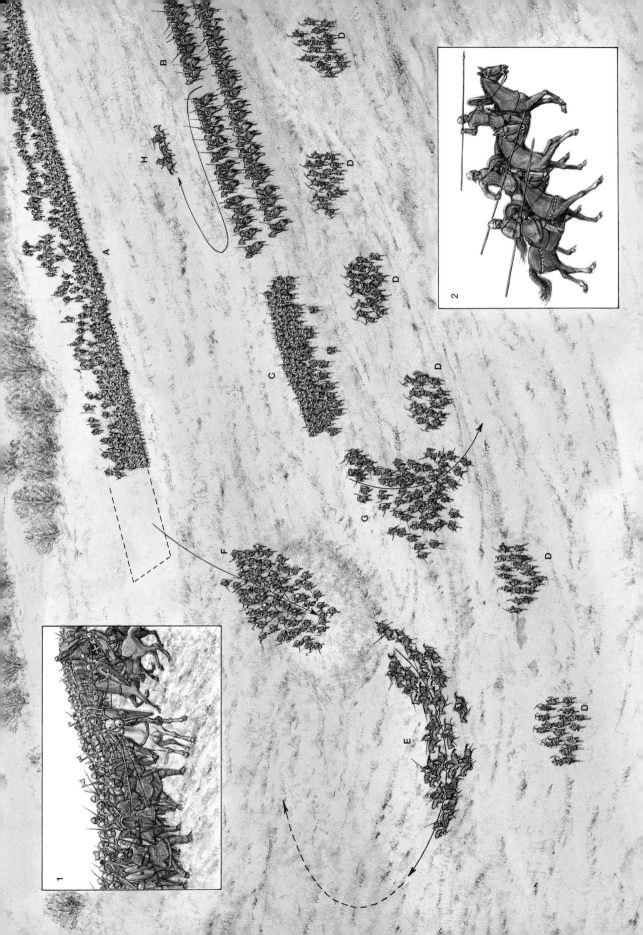

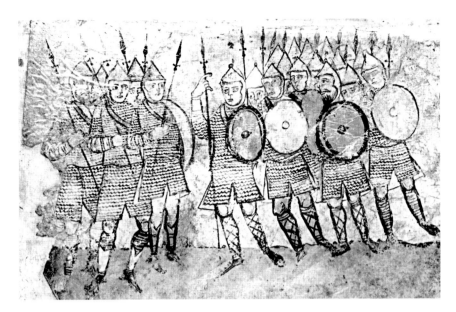

Heavy infantry of the Holy Roman Emperor's army, depicted on a southern Italian manuscript made between AD 981 and 987. (*Exultet Roll from S. Vicenzo al Volturno*, Vatican Library, Rome)

foot defending themselves with large shields held close together. A battle might start with archery in an attempt to weaken such a 'shield-wall' or 'shield-fort', but this would always be followed by man-to-man close combat. Infantry skills remained remarkably consistent until the 11th century, with the sword-armed, shield-carrying footsoldier remaining an élite until the Norman Conquest. The slinging of one's shield on one's back was regarded as particularly brave, and may have been the reality behind the otherwise poetic concept of the bare-chested or *berserk* warrior. The actual fighting seems to have consisted of short periods of close hewing followed by pauses for breath. The power of blows rather than their speed or number was apparently admired, and as a result enormous injuries could be inflicted, especially on the opponent's unshielded legs. (Even in the late 12th century, one of a series of carved panels in Verona illustrating the *Epic of Roland* emphasizes the mythical power of the hero's sword-cut.) The Vikings fought

D BATTLE OF HASTINGS, 1066

This provides a classic example of an army taking advantage of an ill-considered enemy advance, provoked either by a genuine retreat or by the use of the 'feigned-flight' tactic.

King Harold's all-infantry Anglo-Saxon army **(A)** was drawn up along the hilltop, with his élite of armoured *huscarls* forming the centre, and the less well-equipped and less-disciplined *fyrd* on the flanks. Duke William's Norman cavalry **(B)** formed the centre of his line, between infantry flanks **(C)** that were deployed with the most heavily armoured men in front. When not sent forward into action his infantry archers were probably in scattered groups **(D)** behind his battle-line.

The plate represents the moment during the battle when the Breton cavalry on Duke William's left wing **(E)** either broke in retreat after a failed attack, or used a deliberate 'feigned-flight' tactic. As a result, many undisciplined *fyrd* elements from the right wing of the Anglo-Saxon line **(F)** – traditionally the 'offensive' wing of a medieval army – surged downhill in

pursuit. This caused a moment of uncertainty in the Duke's ranks; left-wing Breton infantry **(G)** gave way in the face of the *fyrd* charge, and a rumour spread that Duke William had been killed. He snuffed out this panic by riding out in front of his line and showing himself **(H)**.

His left-wing cavalry **(E)** then wheeled right, to cut the advancing Anglo-Saxons off from their battle-line and destroy them; some of them made a last stand on a small hillock between the armies. King Harold nevertheless had enough control over his men to stop any doomed attempt at rescue.

Inset 1: When Norman cavalry rode up the steep slope against an unbroken part of the Anglo-Saxon shield-wall, their unarmoured horses were vulnerable to the long-handled, large-bladed axes wielded by fully armoured élite *huscarls*.

Inset 2: Norman cavalrymen wielding their lances in three different ways that were still used in the 11th century: from left to right – the couched lance, the underarm swing, and the overarm stab downwards.

A 10th- or early 11th-century Magyar Hungarian helmet of directly riveted iron segments, with the joints highlighted by copper filets. (Archaeological Museum, Pecs; author's photograph)

in the same manner as the Anglo-Saxons, and it is noteworthy that even after cavalry came to predominate in Germany, the Germans and above all the Saxons retained a reputation as sword-fighters.

Equipment

Arms and armour of the Early Medieval period are widely assumed to have been simple, rather uniform and far from abundant. Although this is an oversimplification, it would be correct to say that armour was notably expensive even in prosperous states. Some of the regulations issued by rulers for the equipment that soldiers were expected to acquire may actually have projected an ideal based upon Byzantine practice rather than reflecting what could normally be achieved in an economically stagnant Western Europe. Yet it was not only ideals that came from the Byzantine world; Byzantine styles of military equipment and perhaps significant amounts of weaponry probably reached Central and Western Europe, some penetrating as far as Scandinavia and Iceland. This period similarly witnessed strong military influence from eastern steppe peoples. However, Islamic influence was perhaps more localized, reaching Western Europe via Turkish steppe nomads, or directly from the Middle East, North Africa, the Islamic parts of the Iberian peninsula and from Muslim-ruled Sicily.

Perhaps no aspect of Early Medieval military technology in Europe so obviously reflected differing influences, both internal and external, as did archery. Simple bows more than 6 feet in length – what would now be termed 'longbows' – have been found by archaeologists in various parts of Central and Northern Europe. More significantly, perhaps, in about the 10th century

Armoured riders in close order, representing 'War' in an encyclopedia made for the Carolingian emperor in 1028. (*Encyclopedia of Maurus Hrabanus*, Library, Monastery of Monte Cassino)

there was an associated and quite sudden shift from unbarbed to barbed arrowheads, when European archery changed from being primarily a means of hunting into a technique of warfare. Simple bows were certainly used by the Scandinavian Vikings, and probably also by the mid 11th century Normans. Shorter, so-called 'flat-bows' may have been used in the Carolingian Empire, after Late Roman forms of composite bow apparently fell out of use except in the Mediterranean region. Flat-bows are also said to have been used by the Celtic Welsh, though this is more debatable. Since they were less sensitive to extreme cold than were other simple bows, they were certainly used throughout the medieval period in the far North and sub-Arctic.

The only regions of Western Europe where composite bows seem to have remained in use were the Byzantine Empire and Islamic-influenced Italy, perhaps Islamic-influenced northern Iberia, and of course by the ex-steppe settlers of what is now Hungary. Paradoxically, perhaps, the Magyars themselves appear to have used a larger and in some senses more old-fashioned form of composite bow than did their Avar predecessors. This may again reflect close cultural and military links between the 'forest-steppe' Magyars and the Iranian world; certainly, archaeological evidence shows Magyar bows to have had much in common with those used in the pre-Turkish Islamic Middle East, up to and perhaps even beyond the 11th century.

This figure from an 11th-century carved hunting scene is almost certainly wearing quilted 'soft armour'. (*in situ* Church of St Benedetto, Brindisi; author's photograph)

CAVALRY & CASTLES

The mid 10th to 11th centuries

Though there is evidence for the use of field fortifications and fortified encampments in Western Europe before the 11th century, little is known about them. Despite the fact that Carolingian military regulations made it clear that large armies were expected to erect wooden field fortifications, these may have remained relatively unusual – indeed, it seems that continental Europe's Viking and other invaders often made more effective use of such temporary defences than did the Carolingians. Similarly, the defence of fortified positions remained largely passive throughout the Early Medieval period in Western Europe, with little effort being made to engage the besiegers in an effective manner. Only by making sorties and fighting against direct assault did the defenders normally come into face-to-face contact with their attackers.

That being said, the unified Carolingian Empire of the 8th and early 9th centuries proved itself very effective when dealing with wide-ranging strategic problems. Carolingian armies made some remarkably ambitious and usually (though not invariably) successful long-range campaigns. The fragmentation of the Carolingian Empire saw the rulers of newly emerged states, such as the Kingdom of France, enjoying notably less authority, military or otherwise, than some of their Carolingian predecessors. Warfare degenerated into often very

'Christ Triumphant over the Beasts of the Apocalypse', showing Jesus as a warrior wearing an early form of mail *hauberk*, slit at the sides and primarily intended for infantry combat. (*Chasse de St Hadelin*, Collegiate Church, Visé)

localized conflicts, characterized by squabbles between neighbouring lords in which an often merely nominal central government could not intervene effectively.

Much the same pattern was seen in Germany and Italy following the break-up of the Carolingian Empire. The only real difference was a continuing reliance upon infantry in German border warfare against pagan Slav tribes, but even here armoured cavalry increased in importance from the mid 10th century onwards. By the 11th century it was only in fringe areas that infantry continued to play a dominant military role. Elsewhere, warfare came to be dominated by horsemen, either as mounted infantry or true cavalry – though unfortunately it is often difficult in the sources to distinguish between the two. When mounted archers are mentioned, then these were almost certainly mounted infantry. There was, in fact, no longer a tradition of horse-archery in Western or Central Europe, with the notable and dramatic exception of the newly arrived Magyar Hungarians.

In Germany a new Imperial dynasty, the Ottonians, took over the mantle of the Carolingians, and in time launched a number of ambitious campaigns, several of them south of the Alps in Italy. These were efforts to maintain Imperial authority in a country that was rapidly slipping out of the Holy Roman Emperor's actual, if not yet nominal, control. Such expeditionary forces normally assembled in Bavaria before crossing the Brenner Pass and reassembling in Lombardy; other German armies from Swabia used the St Gothard Pass, while those from Burgundy used the Mont Cenis Pass. Other evidence points to the Ottonians' continued employment of footsoldiers well into the 11th century, though by then they largely operated in support of the cavalry, who had achieved military pre-eminence.

E **BATTLE OF BRÉMULE, 1119**

In this small-scale but decisive battle, most of an out-numbered force of knights dismounted to fight in a defensive line, and defeated two attacks by mounted knights.

The axis of the battle was an old Roman road **(A)**, which passed between thick woods **(B)** close to the stockaded farmstead of Brémule **(C)**. Here a small army of Norman and Anglo-Norman knights, under King Henry I of England and his candidate as duke of Normandy, William Adelin, awaited a larger French force commanded by King Louis VI and his candidate for the dukedom, Guillaume Clito. Most of King Henry's knights **(D)** dismounted, with some archers and crossbowmen in support, to fight a defensive battle. Their horses were taken to the rear **(E)**, where they were guarded by squires, servants and some cavalry, but a small vanguard remained in the saddle.

A charge by the first French *bataille* of 80 knights under William Crespin broke through the Anglo-Norman mounted vanguard, driving it back; William Crespin pressed on to attack

King Henry, but he and his men were defeated, and most were taken to the rear as prisoners **(F)**. The disordered survivors of the Anglo-Norman mounted vanguard **(G)** re-formed to some extent and got forward again, but they were completely shattered by the charge of the second French *bataille* **(H)**, consisting of French feudal lords; this is approximately the moment represented by the main plate. This second French division then also attacked the dismounted Anglo-Norman line, but were defeated in their turn. As a result, the third French *bataille* **(I)** under King Louis retreated, whereupon the Anglo-Norman knights remounted and pursued them.

Inset 1: The ideal of two close-packed *conrois* formations of armoured knights, with lances lowered and held couched, coming into head-to-head contact. Casualties would nevertheless have been small, as the closing speed was low.

Inset 2: Plan of the battlefield, showing the three French *batailles*, and the breaking of the Anglo-Norman cavalry vanguard. (At top left, Norman scouts are shown in the hamlet of Verclive.)

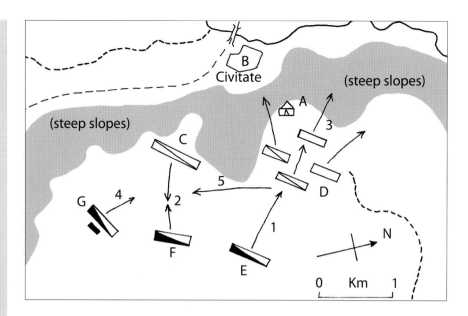

Battle of Civitate, 18 June 1053, in which the Norman conquerors of southern Italy, under the Count of Apulia, defeated an army twice their strength fighting on behalf of Pope Leo IX. The Papal army consisted of Swabian-German, Italian, and Lombard south Italian troops, led by Duke Gerard of Lorraine and Prince Rudolf of Benevento.

Initial dispositions: (**A**) Camp of Papal forces; (**B**) Pope Leo IX in town of Civitate; (**C**) Swabians in extended position on Papal right flank; (**D**) Italians and Lombard cavalry and infantry under Prince Rudolf, on Papal left flank; (**E**) Forces under Richard of Aversa on Norman right flank; (**F**) Forces under Count of Apulia in Norman centre; (**G**) Forces under Robert Guiscard, supported by 'Slavic' infantry, on Norman left.

Movements: (**1**) Normans under Richard of Aversa attack Italians and Lombards; (**2**) Normans under Count of Apulia clash with Swabians on top of small hill, and are forced back; (**3**) Italians and Lombards flee; (**4**) Normans under Robert Guiscard come to assist Humphrey of Hauteville; (**5**) Normans under Richard of Aversa strike Swabians in flank and rear, resulting in their defeat.

During the 10th century those German armies that faced the Magyars often tried to lure their more nimble foes into close combat, and detailed accounts of battles in 10th-century Italy similarly show post-Carolingian forces using ambush tactics and battlefield reserves. Italy also faced a continuing threat from Islamic seaborne raiding, and despite their domestic rivalries the seemingly fragmented local powers generally combined to defeat such invaders. In fact, local Italian forces eventually showed themselves to be more effective than the local defence forces of Northern Europe were proving against a comparable Viking threat.

Eastern and Central Europe

Unlike many other invaders of 10th-century Europe, the Magyar Hungarians changed their military objectives after taking control of the extensive Hungarian Plain. From then on they raided solely for booty, not apparently for conquest. Furthermore, as soon as they themselves were threatened by Imperial German and Kievan Russian armies during the late 10th and early 11th centuries, these Hungarians started to adopt Western European defensive strategies, this being particularly apparent along the western and north-eastern frontiers of their new kingdom. To the south, Hungarian strategy remained more offensive, because here they faced relatively primitive Balkan Slav tribes whose forces still consisted largely of infantry. The change from offensive to defensive strategy in 11th-century Hungary is widely assumed to have led to a significant downgrading of traditional Magyar light cavalry. However, while this may have been true in the west of the kingdom, it did not apply in the eastern provinces; nor would it have been entirely true of the still pastoral, if no longer semi-nomadic, peoples of the Great Plain of central Hungary.

During the 11th century, and probably earlier, the Magyars are described as using wagons to protect their camps, a practice that again recalls the Huns and Sassanians rather than Turkish steppe nomads. In other respects Magyar tactics have generally been regarded as typical of Central Asian steppe peoples, although the Magyars do not fall squarely within that group. Having emerged from the forest-and-steppe fringes of what is now Russia, their horse-archery tactics again seem to have had more in common with the shower-shooting of the earlier Sassanian Persians and contemporary Islamic armies than with the harassment tactics of truly nomadic Turco-Mongol steppe peoples. For their part, the Byzantines had regarded early Magyars as particularly dangerous when retreating, since they made considerable use of feigned flights. They were also described as being capable of switching from the use of bow to the use of the spear and back again at a moment's notice (an ability startlingly reminiscent of the skills expected of a fully trained member of the Islamic military élite).

In Poland, the archaeological record suggests that warfare was dominated by spear-armed infantry until the 10th century, when there seems to have been a sudden rise in the importance of archery. Even then, however, relatively few men were mounted, as was also the case amongst western Slavs closer to the German frontier. Further south, the Balkan Slavs were widely regarded as tactically backward, relying on ambushes in densely forested country, or upon rapid raiding in which their recognized skills in riverine warfare gave them some advantage.

An 11th-century ivory chess-piece from southern Italy or Sicily, showing one swordsman from a 'shield-wall'. (Cabinet des Médailles, Bib. Nationale, Paris)

Northern Europe

Infantry clearly dominated warfare in Anglo-Saxon England until the very end of the Anglo-Saxon state in 1066. Nevertheless, the strategy employed against Vikings invaders – primarily by the Kingdom of Wessex – eventually proved successful. Because the Norse invaders came by sea and often penetrated far up many of England's rivers, the Anglo-Saxons put considerable effort into the securing of river crossings by constructing nearby fortifications. Where possible rivers were also blocked with fortified bridges, which again became vital defensive features. The same strategy would be seen in many northern and western coastal regions of France. Smaller field armies of professional troops, often including a substantial number of mounted infantry if not yet true cavalry, played a similarly important role in harassing or confronting Viking invaders. Such forces would equally feature in frontier warfare against the Celtic states in Wales and Scotland.

Land warfare in Scandinavia and the rest of the Baltic region was essentially similar to that in England, both still being rooted in early Germanic

The Norman army during the early part of the battle of Hastings in 1066, with infantry archers attempting to disrupt the Anglo-Saxon 'shield-wall'. (*Bayeux Tapestry*, Tapestry Museum, Bayeux)

and Scandinavian tribal infantry traditions. The Scandinavian peoples were, however, far more innovative when campaigning overseas. By seizing horses wherever they could, Viking raiders achieved a strategic mobility that was sometimes superior to that of defending forces in England. Similarly, Viking encampments were often protected by ditches and palisades formidable enough to repel Anglo-Saxon infantry. While serving as gathering-points for marauding armies as they spread out to ravage and loot, such fortified encampments could force French and German cavalry to attack them on foot. The situation within Scandinavia was different, with the Norwegians reportedly making a greater use of archery, particularly in the opening stages of a battle and in sea warfare. Archery was also apparent in other Scandinavian and Baltic countries, especially in areas where substantial cavalry forces did not appear until the 12th century.

The Iberian peninsula

Little is known in detail of the strategy adopted by the small Christian states of northern Iberia. The idea that Early Medieval 'barbarian' infantry armies gradually evolved into the largely cavalry forces of the High Middle Ages is clearly erroneous. Until the 11th century, Christian Spanish warfare was largely modelled on that of the Muslim Andalusians, with high-speed raiding by light cavalry being the main form of offensive operation. As early as the 9th century, as the Kingdom of Asturias slowly emerged from its original mountain retreat, a major expedition under the king or a leading nobleman, or by the men of an individual town, was called a *fonsado* or *fossato*, while a smaller cavalry raid was an *algarada*. The primary function of infantry was to defend towns, fortified *castrae* and villages. Essentially the same

terminology was used in 10th- and 11th-century León and Castile, though on a larger and more ambitious scale. However, a *fonsado* would not be a purely cavalry operation if an enemy town was to be attacked or battle with a large enemy army was expected. A larger-scale offensive under royal authority was termed a *hueste*, while *apellido* was a defensive levée-en-masse in the face of enemy invasion. The *cavalgada*, *algara*, *corredura* or *azaria* were all small raids into enemy territory. Two overall types of war were recognized, *guerra* being an internal conflict between Christians, while *bellum* was 'holy war' against the Muslims. It is worth noting that the high plains of La Mancha and Extramadura in Spain were not then the cereal-growing regions they are today, but were characterized by sheep-ranching, raiding and rustling. Meanwhile both Christians and Muslims made great efforts to control the passes through the sequence of mountain ranges that straddled the Iberian peninsula roughly from east to west.

Normans and French

The Norman attitude to warfare was somewhat different. By the 11th century, Norman armies were already noted for their discipline, and their commanders for remarkable patience. Norman warfare was characterized by careful reconnaissance, prolonged sieges and blockades, occasional battles that were usually associated with such sieges, and a preference for diplomacy whenever possible. Negotiation was clearly regarded as being better than the unnecessary spilling of blood, especially if that blood belonged to the military élite. An ability to carry out winter campaigns was characteristic, with consequent close attention to the security of supplies and supply lines, and a willingness to retreat when circumstances were unfavourable. The Normans' considerable

The two-handed, long-handled axe, typically carried by the armoured *huscarls* in the centre of King Harold's battle array, inflicted terrible damage on the attacking Norman cavalry at Hastings. (*Bayeux Tapestry*, Tapestry Museum, Bayeux)

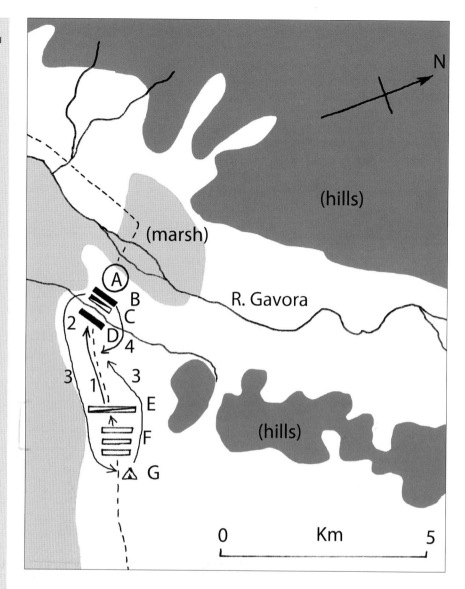

Battle of Zallaqa, 23 October 1086, in which King Alfonso VI of León amd Castile was defeated by a coalition of Muslim armies under the *Murabitun* ruler Yusuf Ibn Tashfin. Perhaps separated by, or partially hidden within, a dry stream-bed, the Murabit army consisted largely of mounted troops from Morocco, Mauretania and Senegal; in the rear were élite African infantry armed with javelins. Arriving along the main road from Toledo, the Christians broke an agreed truce for Muslim Friday prayers, and launched a massive cavalry assault. The Muslims relied upon early Islamic defensive tactics, with largely dismounted Andalusian forces under al-Mu'tamid Ibn Abbad of Seville in their front line.

Initial dispositions:
(**A**) Muslim encampment;
(**B**) African infantry rearguard;
(**C**) Murabit centre;
(**D**) Andalusian vanguard;
(**E**) Castilian cavalry;
(**F**) Castilian infantry;
(**G**) Castilian camp.

Movements: (**1**) Castilians launch a sudden attack at dawn; (**2**) Andalusians suffer significant losses, but hold the line with support from a small Murabit unit. (**3**) Yusuf Ibn Tashfin launches a flanking attack – though on which flank is unknown; this burns the Castilian camp, and attacks Castilians from behind; (**4**) Castilians start to break; African infantry attack and complete the rout – again, the flank is unknown.

use of espionage, and efforts to identify potential traitors within an enemy's ranks, were also typical of their pragmatic attitude towards warfare.

The Normans were similarly careful when it came to offensive operations. For example, Duke William's invasion of England in 1066 was a classic case of the use of a well-balanced combined army of cavalry and infantry. William's uncharacteristic decision to risk all at the battle of Hastings on 14 October probably reflected the fact that the Anglo-Saxons threatened to hem in the Norman beachhead, which was also vulnerable to being cut off by sea. Ferocious ravaging of Anglo-Saxon territory after the Normans' victory at Hastings was the normal sequel to such a battlefield success, as were the Anglo-Saxons' attempts at guerrilla resistance. This was in turn countered by the Norman policy of castle-building, a focus on controlling all main towns and roads, and William's holding of senior Anglo-Saxon figures as hostages. In reality it was not the epic battle on Senlac Hill that brought Anglo-Saxon England to its knees, but the Normans' subsequent ruthless campaign of ravaging recalcitrant territories.

The Normans clearly used archery to weaken an enemy at the start of a battle. As seen as Hastings, these archers were followed (or perhaps more correctly, defended) by armoured infantry, who might themselves also attack the enemy line. However, the main offensive role in Norman armies fell to the cavalry. Norman commanders certainly made use of the feigned-flight tactic, which might have been brought home by Norman troops who fought against more sophisticated Byzantine and Muslim foes in southern Italy. On the other hand, there is strong evidence to suggest that this tactic had persisted in France since Roman times.

South of the English Channel, the 11th century witnessed the start of more than a hundred years of sometimes grim campaigning by the kings of France in prolonged efforts to take control of turbulent regional centres of power. Even so, during the first half of that century the warlike career of a great regional lord like Fulk Nera of Anjou included remarkably few full-scale battles; the provincial warfare of this period remained largely a matter of raiding, ravaging, besieging or defending fortified locations.

The earliest medieval Western European illustrations of hand-held crossbows are found in southern Europe, and usually depict them in the hands of devils; this example dates from 1096. (*in situ* Cathedral of St Sernin, Toulouse; author's photograph)

By the 11th century both French and Normans were famed as lance-armed cavalry, and used couched lances in *conrois* formations, ideally in multiples of ten men. It is important to note that, unlike earlier rapid attack-and-withdrawal tactics, the cavalry's horses now walked into the charge. They avoided trotting, which was uncomfortable for an armoured rider in the new style of peaked saddle and using long stirrup-leathers, and was also tiring for the horse. For the final part of a charge the *conrois* went into a slow canter rather than a gallop.

The crossbow

In Western European warfare as a whole, the re-emergence of the hand-held crossbow was of considerable significance. It had almost certainly survived since Late Roman times as a hunting weapon in some areas, but this very early crossbow seems to have been unsuited to the small-scale, largely skirmishing warfare that characterized the Early Medieval period in Western Europe. However, an increase in siege warfare in some areas during the 10th and more particularly the 11th century resulted in the reappearance of crossbows in the hands of a small number of infantry. Islamic influence cannot be ruled out in this respect, whereas the Byzantines – rather surprisingly – do not seem to have played a part. Subsequent 11th-century improvements to the hand-held crossbow may have reflected indigenous economic and technological advances, or the introduction of ideas from other parts of the world. One of the most significant may have been a wider use of pole-lathes, which enabled accurate revolving crossbow release-nuts to be manufactured in larger quantities. Amongst more northerly peoples the Normans adopted this weapon with enthusiasm during the second half of the 11th century, though they were not alone in this. The fact that early crossbows did not entirely oust the ordinary bow as an infantry weapon may be explained by the fact that they could not be aimed effectively beyond a range of 80 yards/metres, since raising the end of the stock or tiller to allow for the arrow's drop simply obscured the target from the bowman's view.

THE SUPPOSED DOMINANCE OF CAVALRY

The 12th to mid 13th centuries

The still widespread popular view that medieval military leaders lacked both interest and ability in strategy and tactics is at variance with the evidence – and totally so where the 12th and 13th centuries are concerned. Furthermore, the normal image of medieval warfare as consisting largely of brief but extremely violent clashes of arms is again not entirely correct. During the 12th century, battles occasionally consisted of mutually entrenched camps bombarding each other with stone-throwing engines, while small raiding parties attempted to cut the enemy's supply routes, to attack his foragers if they ranged too far afield, to block roads and defend bridges. Thus the basic imperatives of 12th- and 13th-century European warfare were essentially the same as they had been for many centuries, and would remain so for centuries to come.

There was little change in the skills demanded of cavalry or infantry during this period. The heavy horsemen now relied overwhelmingly on the couched lance, the armoured *conrois* formed by such riders having now become a battlefield 'projectile' in its own right. (The many apparent references to individual combat between champions are likely either to have been a literary convention, or to have referred to the leaders of small units whose followers were also involved in such combats.) But if armoured cavalry dominated warfare throughout most of Christian Western Europe during this period, infantry continued to play vital and perhaps increasingly important roles.

The Franco-Norman heartland

While we should be wary of stereotypes, the classic warfare of this period was most clearly illustrated in the Kingdom of France, including the Angevin provinces ruled by the kings of England. Here armies usually mustered in late spring, assembling at an agreed rendezvous. There is clear evidence of broad strategic planning and forethought, and of considerable efforts to mislead

an enemy as to precisely when and where an attack might be launched. Nevertheless, the nature of medieval warfare often made such campaigns somewhat predictable. Certain castles – for example, Château-Gaillard in Normandy – were built primarily as forward bases and springboards for campaigns into specific enemy regions, so an army seen to be assembling at such a place would have a limited choice of potential objectives.

Campaigns themselves largely focused upon the ravaging and devastation of enemy territory, sometimes combined with attempts to take key castles or fortified towns. The invading army would normally try to avoid the main defending forces, initially by misleading the enemy commander about the invader's intentions. However, the invading forces might attempt to catch the defenders unawares and at a disadvantage, while striving not to be caught in the same way themselves.

A graphic account of one such late 12th-century invading force describes how it was preceded by scouts and incendiaries, who set fire to enemy villages and captured peasants. Then came the foragers, who collected the spoils and loaded them into the army's baggage train, and the primary role of the main fighting forces was to protect such foragers. During these destructive operations, the élite armoured knights would not be riding their expensive

Infantry closely following cavalry units are shown in a stylized manner on this mid 12th-century northern Italian carved capital. Note the two different helmets, one with a nasal and a forward-tilted apex, the other a *spangenhelm* with cheek-pieces; the kite-shaped shields, that of the footsoldier being 'clipped' at the bottom; and the four-tailed banner. (*in situ* Cathedral, Parma; photograph Luca Trascinelli)

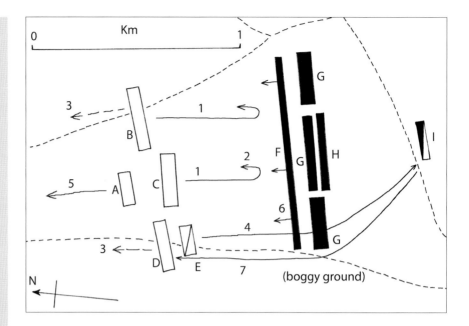

Battle of the Standard, 23 August 1138, in which an Anglo-Norman army under William of Aumale defeated an invading Scottish army led by King David I. The Scots were largely unarmoured; while they broke through or outflanked the Anglo-Norman line, they suffered severe losses from the Anglo-Norman archers, and were unable to make an impact upon the armoured knights.

Initial dispositions: (**A**) King David and household troops; (**B**) Scots from Lothians and West Highlands; (**C**) Allied troops from Kingdom of Galloway; (**D**) Allied troops from Cumbria and Teviot regions; (**E**) Prince Henry with Scots cavalry; (**F**) Vanguard of Anglo-Norman archers and dismounted knights; (**G**) Dismounted Anglo-Norman knights in centre and on flanks; (**H**) English shire levies; (**I**) Horse lines.

Movements: (**1**) Attack by Galwegians and Lothians – and possibly Cumbrians?; (**2**) Galwegians flee after death of two leaders; (**3**) Scottish army starts to fragment; (**4**) Cavalry charge by Prince Henry reaches Anglo-Norman horse lines, but fails to make Anglo-Norman army pull back; (**5**) King David withdraws; (**6**) Anglo-Normans pursue retreating Scots; (**7**) Prince Henry furls his banner to hide his identity, and returns with advancing Anglo-Normans to rejoin King David.

destriers or war-horses, which were only used in battle; nor would they normally wear full armour, this being heavy and tiring, thus reducing the endurance of men and horses. Instead knights and other members of the mounted élite rode *palfreys*, ordinary riding horses. If the cavalry were in dangerous territory they would probably carry their shields, though these would normally remain in the hands of their squires until needed, and the knights would almost certainly not don their helmets until the enemy was either seen or heard. Normally such ravaging armies moved extremely slowly, but even so, élite infantry could cover more than 125 miles/200 kilometres in a week and still be fresh enough to defeat enemy cavalry, while mounted troops could, of course, travel faster over shorter distances. While major pitched battles remained rare, the small-scale skirmishing that characterized most warfare demanded considerable tactical skill.

Traditionally, French or Anglo-Norman cavalry were deployed in *batailles* or divisions, according to their place or province of origin, and normally under the leadership of the senior count or duke of the area in question. Large divisions would, in turn, consist of *echelles* or squadrons. The exact relationship between an *echelle* and a *bataille* is unclear, though the *batailles* were certainly subdivided into small *conrois* sections as they had been since Carolingian times. The *conrois* itself now normally consisted of about 20–24 knights in two or three ranks, riding very close together, shoulder-to-shoulder in a manner described as *seréement*. The separate *conrois* also appear to have ridden quite close to one another. Whether a theoretical tactical unit of ten men (known in early 12th-century England as a *constabularium*) was actually used in battle is again unknown.

The tactical function of these densely packed units was to act as shock cavalry – the 'shock' that their charges delivered being largely psychological, as was almost always the case throughout the history of cavalry warfare. They charged at a relatively slow speed, and, if they succeeded in breaking the enemy's formation, they would then fight individually in the resulting *mêlée*. Ideally, a 12th- or 13th-century heavy cavalry charge hoped to break right through an enemy line, then turn and charge once more from the rear. It is clear that there was also use of operational reserves, intended to take advantage of any such break in the enemy's front. Such reserves were – like most other 'ambush' forces in the typical tactics of the French and neighbouring peoples during this period – almost always cavalry. They could also be thrown against an enemy's flank if the opportunity arose, particularly if this could be done unexpectedly and from cover. It is also clear that 12th-century Franco-Norman and Anglo-Norman cavalry continued to make use of feigned retreats.

The border regions

There were several distinctly different strategic and tactical traditions in what might be described as the frontier areas of Christendom. The most obvious difference was usually a relative lack of armoured cavalry in the most distant fringes of Europe. In many cases warfare in such marginal regions was characterized by an even less frequent resort to full-scale battle. For example, warfare in the Baltic region had several features in common with that in the Celtic fringe regions. During the Northern Crusades, the invading Scandinavians and Germans enjoyed an initial rush of relatively easy conquests, but thereafter they found it necessary to adopt much the same strategy of raid and ambush as their Lithuanian and other Baltic opponents had used for centuries. The forces of all those involved were particularly vulnerable when returning home burdened with booty and rustled cattle.

By the 13th century, the German invaders had developed a sophisticated system of small stone fortifications or blockhouses from which they could launch raids, ambush enemy raiders, and gradually consolidate their hold over captured territory. In response, the Prussians, Lithuanians and other indigenous peoples made skilful use of light-cavalry guerrilla tactics in

This 12th-century northern Italian carved typanum shows the infantry of the urban militia of Verona. (*in situ* Church of St Zeno, Verona; author's photograph)

marshes and forests. These were referred to as *latrunculi* or *strutere*, 'banditry or destruction', and were used both against the Crusader invaders and by local warriors serving them as auxiliaries after having accepted Christian domination. Further north, the nomadic Karelian Lapps were noted for their skill in winter raiding. Small groups of Karelian warriors wearing skis attacked isolated enemy outposts, though not the more densely populated centres to the west.

Within Eastern Europe the armies of countries such as Poland appear to have used a mixture of Western and Eastern – or more particularly, Russian – strategy and tactics. In contrast, Bohemia was now fully within the Western European military tradition of Germany. Hungarian commanders seem to have tried to use Western European strategies while still having to rely upon a large proportion of troops equipped and skilled in their own non-Western tradition. The same was true of the Balkan states, where Hungarian, Western, Byzantine and Central Asian steppe influences came into contact and fusion.

Throughout the medieval period the sparsely inhabited Anglo-Scottish Borders were a zone of transition. Although the exact position of the national frontier itself was known to those involved, it had little bearing on local warfare. The Borders remained a relatively quiet area during the 12th and 13th centuries, with little raiding by local people. The only major disruptions seem to have been caused by the royal armies of each kingdom either trying to move the frontier to their own king's advantage, or when passing through the Borders on their way to attack the enemy's major centres to the north or south. Even when larger campaigns took place there seem to have been few attempts by small local castle garrisons to attack the enemy's extended lines of communication. The normal responses to aggression were counter-invasion, counter-raid and retaliation.

Within Scotland itself, however, internal warfare seems to have had a great deal in common with that of Celtic Ireland, being characterized by small-scale raiding and cattle-rustling that caused relatively low casualties. The Irish themselves continued to limit warfare to such harrying tactics; one sub-king or prince might attempt to dominate a neighbour, but his forces generally

F | BATTLE OF LEGNANO, 1176

This was an example of the successful co-operation of northern Italian communal infantry and cavalry. The battle almost certainly took place on open ground between the villages of Borsano and Legnano.

Earlier in the day, the German (Imperial) cavalry of the Emperor Frederick I Barbarossa had defeated the Lombard League cavalry north of the battlefield, and the latter fled southwards beyond the League's field fortifications at Borsano (A). The all-cavalry Imperial army (B) then pressed the Lombard League infantry, including making assaults on their palisades, for which some riders probably dismounted. The Italian militia (C) were in close-packed 'phalanx' formations, defending stockades around the ox-drawn *carroccio* 'banner cart' of Milan (D). Each Milanese infantry unit was drawn from a specific 'gate' or quarter of that city, and there were others from allied cities.

Meanwhile, the Lombard League cavalry joined forces with an allied contingent of cavalry from Brescia, and returned to the battlefield, apparently unseen by the Imperial army until it was too late. The returning League cavalry (E) charged into the Imperial cavalry from the rear and flank, and the Brescians (F) penetrated deeply enough to attack Emperor Frederick's bodyguard and unhorse the emperor himself. Thinking he had been killed, the Imperial army then fled, pursued westwards by League cavalry as far as the Ticino river.

Inset 1: The ranks of a Milanese militia infantry phalanx, based on northern Italian art from this period. The front rank are heavily armoured men with spears and long shields; less well-armoured men, also with spears and long shields, form the second rank; the third rank are lightly armoured men with swords and small shields, and the rear rank archers and crossbowmen.

Inset 2: Detail of a close-packed *conrois* formation of fully armoured cavalry, charging with lances lowered and held in the couched position, with slightly less well-equipped mounted sergeants close behind. They are followed by a line of largely unarmoured squires leading spare war-horses.

tried to avoid killing too many of the enemy. It was these people, rather than their land, whom the king was either attempting to dominate or from whom he wished to exact tribute. In such warfare the most effective strategy still appears to have been cattle-rustling, and the stolen beasts were generally returned to their owners once the latter submitted. Those on the receiving end of these tactics would rely on a highly developed *rabhadh* 'alarm' system, intended to provide time for the people and their herds to reach a place of safety. If this failed, the defenders would try to ambush the enemy as they made their way home, slowed down by the captured cattle. As a result the rearguard rather than the vanguard was generally regarded as a place of honour in traditional Celtic Irish warfare.

During the 12th and 13th centuries the main preoccupation of Welsh warfare was defence against English aggression, which resulted in the sort of prolonged guerrilla conflict that was otherwise rare in the Middle Ages. Welsh forces would attempt to harass and ambush the Anglo-Norman supply trains, particularly in wooded, marshy or mountainous terrain, but they rarely attempted to meet more heavily armed enemies in open battle. Above all, the Welsh commanders tried to predict and then block an enemy's line of withdrawal, or to force him down a specific route by blocking all others. In response, the Anglo-Normans tried to lure the Welsh into ambushes, often by pretending to retreat in disorder. Meanwhile the Welsh developed a talent for night-fighting; profited from bad weather that limited Anglo-Norman operations to the coasts and valleys; and adopted some more modern cavalry skills from their adversaries. Unlike the Irish, the Welsh sometimes carried out a scorched-earth policy in the face of the more determined English invasions.

A late 12th- or very early 13th-century Italian chronicle of the fall of the Norman Kingdom of Sicily illustrates fully armoured knights, unarmoured archers, helmeted crossbowmen, and war-galleys. (*Liber ad Honorem Augusti* by Petrus de Ebulo, Burgerbibliothek, Cod. 120.II, f.131r, Berne)

CAVALRY & INFANTRY COMBINATIONS

Although armoured cavalry remained the dominant élite in most Western European armies, the strategy and tactics of the later 12th and first half of the 13th centuries demanded the recruitment of many other military specialists. Furthermore, it would be wrong to regard those non-élite, largely infantry troops who carried out the process of ravaging and devastation merely as a homogenous rabble; they seem to have included men with specific skills, such as foragers, incendiaries, and heavier infantry to guard the supply train. The role of mounted troops might include similarly specific skills, though a fully trained knight would presumably have been capable of undertaking all duties. The reality during this period was that armoured cavalry may have dominated the battlefield, but not warfare in the wider sense.

While battles fought entirely by cavalry, very rare during the 12th century, may have become slightly more common in the 13th century, most battles still involved both horse and foot. Light infantry continued to use javelins, particularly the *dardiers* of Gascony and several other parts of southern France. In most core regions of Europe the javelin was no longer regarded as suitable for a member of the military élite, though early 13th-century Germany might have been something of an exception, with references to knights continuing to use such weapons when on foot. Here and elsewhere knights were fully prepared to break the shafts of their lances in order to have a shorter spear suitable for fighting on foot. Under such circumstances they are described as advancing on foot still in essentially the same closely ordered *conrois* formations as they used when on horseback.

The differences between heavy and light infantry were less clear-cut than they would be in the 14th century, but even so, well-armoured men would presumably have been better suited to static tasks such as defending river crossings and fixed positions, or providing a defensive shield for more lightly equipped foragers. In such cases the infantry were normally supported by cavalry. In other respects, infantry tactics are recorded in less detail than those of the horsemen, and the little that is known applies to heavy infantry. The evidence for lighter footsoldiers indicates that their main role would have been to harass an enemy and perhaps launch ambushes, sometimes in combination with cavalry. Evidence from the 12th century describes heavier infantry being drawn up in three divisions behind a defensive ditch, but still remaining vulnerable to flank attack by enemy cavalry. To defend themselves from this danger, in the absence of their own cavalry wings infantry would try to anchor their flanks on natural obstacles or topographical features, or adopt a 'crown' formation for all-round defence.

The little information available concerning field fortifications suggests that, again, there had been no great changes since the 11th century. Such defences still consisted of ditches, earth banks or ramparts, wooden palisades or iron-pointed wooden stakes. The existence of the latter, however, clearly indicates forethought, and the preparation of perhaps reusable field fortifications before the start of a campaign.

Italian militias

In Italy, infantry warfare was more advanced and more disciplined than elsewhere in Christian Europe, the Italians' only real rivals being found in Islamic Andalusia. Northern Italian militia forces were described as fighting in close-ordered ranks, with their city's *carroccio* or 'banner-wagon' forming a rallying point and a refuge for the wounded, and with their flanks covered by cavalry. These men used long spears almost as pikes against the enemy's largely unarmoured horses – a tactic that demanded considerable discipline, but that often proved capable of stopping a cavalry charge. Nevertheless, even the highly disciplined infantry of the northern Italian cities needed the support of armoured cavalry, and horse and foot clearly fought as an integrated team. A noted example was at the battle of Legnano in 1176, where the Milanese infantry militia fought the Emperor's German cavalry to a standstill, thus giving their own cavalry time to reform and launch a successful counter-attack (see Plate F). In another battle, that at Carcano in 1160, the cavalry of Lombardy earned widespread praise for their discipline and restraint, in remaining to support their infantry instead of charging off in pursuit of broken enemy horsemen.

The most prestigious and highly paid Italian infantry of this period were clearly crossbowmen. The first crossbow mercenaries to be recorded in substantial numbers during the 12th century seem to have been Genoese from northern Italy and Gascons from south-western France. As yet they were still often associated with ordinary hand-bow archers; in 1181 Genoa itself sent only ten crossbowmen accompanying 200 other archers to support neighbouring Alessandria. However, by the first half of the 14th century these crossbow-armed Italian infantrymen would become the most renowned mercenaries of their day.

By the early 13th century the French king's army, which was widely regarded as an almost ideal pattern by many other rulers, included various military professionals in addition to the knights: mounted sergeants, mounted crossbowmen, infantry sergeants, infantry crossbowmen, and sappers or engineers. The obvious increase in the importance of infantry throughout most of Western Europe was not a consequence of lessons learned during the Crusades, but rather a continuous development of what had been happening since the 11th century.

Archery

The increasing importance of archers, and more particularly of crossbowmen, may have been in response to the increasing effectiveness of the armoured cavalry charge, even though crossbowmen had initially appeared as a consequence of more frequent siege warfare. Such infantry were more effective than is generally recognized, even if in open battle they still usually needed the support of cavalry. Similarly, their morale often needed stiffening through the presence of dismounted knights. In France the simple bow was not ousted

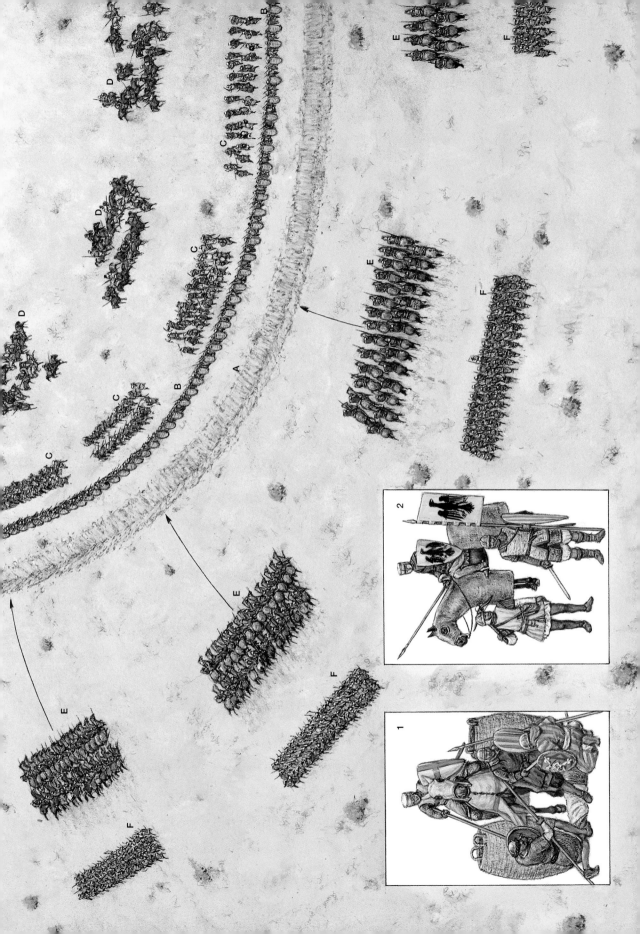

as a war-weapon by the crossbow until the early 13th century, but during that century the élite of professional crossbowmen were already mounted (though they probably fought on foot, and should be classed as mounted infantry).

Tactics naturally varied according to circumstances, but in Anglo-Norman warfare it now seems to have been normal for cavalry to advance in very close-ordered ranks, with infantry archers and crossbowmen on their flanks. The role of such infantry was to injure as many of the enemy's horses as possible. When fighting in defence against a cavalry attack, the infantry were often supported by their own fully armoured but dismounted knights. Under some circumstances these knights would also advance against the enemy on foot and in close-ordered ranks. Other evidence indicates that, again in a defensive situation, the archers might be placed in front of dismounted knights, with mounted knights behind them, and sometimes with mounted-infantry archers on the left flank; the latter were expected to hurry to a new position from which they could shoot at the advancing enemy's unshielded right side.

The similarity between such tactics and those of traditional pre-Turkish, Arab-Islamic armies – such as those of 10th-and 12th-century Egypt or pre-Norman Sicily, North Africa and southern Spain – is striking. Some degree of Arab-Islamic influence upon the Normans seems likely,

Full mail horse-armour depicted in an early 13th-century Brabantine manuscript. ('First Book of Maccabees' in the *Bible de Léau*, Bib. du Grand Seminaire, Ms. 1B3, Liège)

perhaps via Spain or Sicily. Similarly, the death of the standard-bearer or the fall of his flag almost invariably signalled defeat in Anglo-Norman or French battles, precisely as it did in earlier and contemporary Arab-Islamic warfare.

Meanwhile the simple bow, used so effectively by the Norman conquerors in 1066, never disappeared in England, where it would later attain almost mythic significance, being incorrectly called the 'longbow' by later historians. More surprisingly, perhaps, some mid 13th-century Norwegian knights were described as being skilled archers on horseback, though in hunting rather than warfare. Quite how that skill reached Scandinavia remains unknown, but it might have been brought back by Scandinavian warriors who had earlier served in the Byzantine Emperor's Varangian Guard.

Northern and Eastern Europe

The renowned light cavalry of the early 12th-century Baltic coastal Slavs, and of other eastern Baltic peoples such as the Lithuanians and Prussians, rode lighter horses than their German and Scandinavian Crusader enemies. Little is known of their combat skills at this time, though the mid 13th-century

Lithuanians are said to have fought much like the Mongols, but with javelins rather than bows. During the 12th century the Slav tribes of the southern Baltic coast had made great use of infantry archers, but these soon found themselves outclassed by the apparently larger bows and more powerful crossbows of Danish invaders. Perhaps these Slav archers were using a form of the short or 'flat-bow' characteristic of the Lapps far to their north. Light infantry axes also appear to have been characteristic of the Lithuanians.

Whereas armoured knightly cavalry remained dominant in most of Europe, there were again clear variations in several border or backward areas. In Poland, for example, contemporary descriptions indicate that the military élite in the west of the country differed from that of the eastern provinces, largely in the west's greater number of spear-armed and armoured horsemen. In Hungary, an élite trained in Western methods of warfare may already have formed a majority of cavalry by the end of the 12th century. Unfortunately, little information survives about the tactics used by the remaining Hungarian light cavalry; but their continued use of traditional weapons such as the composite bow, and their wearing of only light or no armour, suggests that they too relied on traditional harassment tactics. To the south, in Croatia, Western European military styles dominated completely, but poisoned arrows were recorded in the hands of Serb archers.

Norway was a relatively backward part of Europe during the High Medieval period, and its mid 13th-century art often showed cavalrymen with large, old-fashioned shields and simple *chapel-de-fer* helmets. ('The Story of St Mary of Antioch', *in situ* wooden parish church at Ål; photograph Jo. Sellaeg)

The Celtic fringe

Among those fringe areas where most men still fought predominantly on foot, several distinctive infantry tactics were developed, though few were as effective as those of northern Italy. When in open terrain, for example, the Scots used the *schiltron*, an essentially circular formation of massed spearmen all facing outwards. The men involved do not appear to have been as disciplined or as manoeuvrable as their Italian counterparts, nor were their spears yet as long as later medieval or Early Modern pikes.

Northern Welsh spear-armed infantry sometimes fought in a similar manner, but on other occasions Welsh forces are described as placing their cavalry either at the centre or on one flank, or separately upon nearby high ground ready to swoop on the enemy should the opportunity arise. Here light cavalry continued to predominate both numerically and tactically, yet the Welsh soon adopted some aspects of Anglo-Norman horsemanship and, like their enemies, were fully prepared to fight on foot when necessary. Tactically, they seem to have used sudden and repeated attacks and withdrawals much like Middle Eastern Islamic and some Byzantine cavalry. However, it must be remembered that precisely these tactics had also been used by the Late Roman cavalry on whom the Romano-British predecessors of Welsh light cavalry surely modelled themselves. Perhaps such tactics had never died out in the Celtic west of Britain?

In Celtic Irish armies, small groups of lightly equipped cavalry riding ponies also provided the main striking power. Here it is clear that the foreign mercenaries hired by local rulers could often be classed as heavy infantry – precisely the type of troops that were lacking in marginal areas like Celtic Ireland. (But many Irish footsoldiers still used primitive slings to good effect, especially against Anglo-Norman cavalry horses.)

WARFARE AGAINST EXTERNAL ENEMIES

The 12th to mid 13th centuries

Ecological factors clearly played a part in the strategy developed by the Christian states of the Iberian peninsula during the 12th to 14th centuries. Control of winter and summer pastures was economically and thus militarily important for both Christian and Muslim frontier communities, and this led to specific forms of small-scale campaign.

H **PRELUDE TO THE BATTLE OF PELAGONIA, 1259**

This is an example of the effective use of light cavalry to weaken heavy cavalry before a main engagement even started.

At Pelagonia, the Byzantine Emperor Michael VIII Palaiologos of Nicaea defeated a Latin coalition army formed by the Crusader principality of Achaia, King Manfred of southern Italy, and the Byzantine Despot of Epirus. The battle was preceded by skirmishing that fatally weakened the Latin forces, and the Despot of Epirus had already abandoned the field.

Sources of sufficient drinking water for large numbers of horses were relatively few, making their use predictable. Here, heavy cavalry war-horses **(A)** of the Latin coalition are being watered in a steep-sided gulley by largely unarmed servants and horse-handlers, guarded by a weak detachment of cavalry **(B)**. On the hill above, a stronger guard force of Latin infantry and cavalry **(C)** are being distracted by Nicaean cavalry making a feint attack **(D)**. Under cover of this diversion, a strong Nicaean force of Turkish and Kipchaq horse-archers **(E)** sweep down the gulley to capture or kill the watering horses.

Inset 1: A Kipchaq horse-archer in Byzantine service shooting at a pursuer, and a *turcopole* horse-archer shooting at a low-level target.

Inset 2: A typical Latin (probably Italian) infantry crossbowman, with his *pavesari* shield-bearer.

In Castile, November was the month when the cattle and sheep were assembled at an agreed location, and in December one *esculquero* guard would be put in charge of each herd of cows, with three guards for every flock of sheep. These *esculqueros*, who did not themselves act as herdsmen, elected a leader before moving south into the high plains of La Mancha. They and the animals returned in mid March, the guards being disbanded while the herds were driven into summer pastures on the high Sierras, with a smaller escort of infantry provided by the villagers. A comparable system was used by the Muslims who came up from their winter grazing in the southern Sierras. As a result there were constant clashes and stock-rustling along the most important migration routes, known as *cañadas*. (It has even been suggested that large-scale cattle rustling was virtually invented in 12th-century Toledo.) A similar system developed for herds of pigs, which were protected by guards called *rafaleros*.

In contrast, offensive warfare during the Iberian *Reconquista* varied between small-scale raids, and much larger campaigns of conquest – often to consolidate gains made by persistent raiding. Such operations were carefully planned, and usually took place in the dry summer and autumn, being channelled along main roads, bridges and passes. As a result, major river crossings were invariably defended by castles or fortified towns. Smaller raids could take place at almost any time of year, the main concern of those taking part being to keep their own escape route open. For example, a small 12th-century Castilian army on such a campaign would be divided into two parts: the *azaga* which built and defended an encampment, and an *algara*

A clear depiction of a mixed-arms force. The infantry show a mixture of seemingly archaic northern Spanish and Islamic Andalusian military styles; they are drawn up in a traditional manner, with fully armoured men at the front and unarmoured archers with recurved bows at the rear. (*Beatus of Liébana*, Pierpont Morgan Lib., Ms. 429, New York)

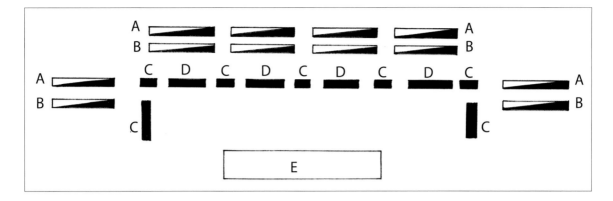

Schematic archetypal 12th-century Crusader battle array. (**A**) Knightly cavalry; (**B**) Mounted sergeants and squires in support; (**C**) Crossbowmen and archers; (**D**) Infantry armed with close-combat weapons; (**E**) Baggage. (After Von Pawlikowski-Cholewa)

which did the actual raiding. The main problem with such a strategy was that it left the army's own place of origin vulnerable to a Muslim counter-raid.

In other respects distinctive tactics developed in Christian Iberia, in an apparent combination of French influences from the north and Muslim from the south, and were then often adopted by both Christians and Muslims. These tactics were characterized by large numbers of relatively light cavalry, usually operating from a strongly fortified encampment defended by large numbers of crossbowmen. On other occasions cavalry might sometimes operate independently, without infantry in direct support; heavier horsemen formed the front rank, with lighter squires or sergeants behind.

Crusader armies

Crusades launched from Europe never abandoned their broader strategic vision. Even the unnumbered Crusade which supposedly 'got lost' before being destroyed in eastern Anatolia in 1101 may have been part of an overconfident bid to conquer Baghdad by following the Tigris river. Thereafter the main strategic hope was to conquer Egypt, though this also failed. On the other hand, most Crusades were launched in response to Muslim successes, and remained essentially reactive rather than proactive.

Throughout most of the 12th century the newly established Crusader states in the Middle East were trapped within a traditional view of their own military superiority vis-a-vis the Muslims, long after this had ceased to be a reality. Not until the later 12th and the 13th century did the Crusader states in Syria and Palestine finally accept the need for caution and a general avoidance of offensive operations, consequently adopting defensive strategies similar to those long favoured by the Byzantine Empire. Furthermore, they had learned the basic truth that the fate of a small, vulnerable region like Palestine was ultimately decided by bigger struggles elsewhere, not even necessarily within Greater Syria. The Crusaders' greatest strategic asset remained divisions amongst their Muslim neighbours, though these could sometimes be mirrored by divisions within their own ranks. Sieges and naval skirmishes were characteristic of warfare between the Crusader states and Byzantium, but in the mid 13th century the Crusaders in both the Middle East and Greece were still capable of making savage and effective counter-raids against their enemies. The most effective were rapid *chevauchée* raids by fast and relatively lightly armoured forces known as *caravans*. During the 13th century these employed varying proportions of heavy cavalry knights, lighter cavalry *turcopoles*, and infantry, such variations probably reflecting what troops were available as much as the nature of the target.

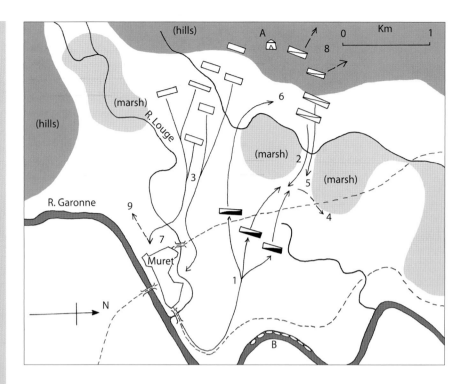

At least as much attention was given to maintaining cohesion on the march as to other aspects of warfare in the Crusader states, probably because relatively slow-moving Western-style forces remained vulnerable to their more rapid and manoeuvrable Eastern foes. As a general rule a rectangular formation was adopted in open country, and a column with strong flank guards in the hills. Before the battle of Hattin in 1187, for example, the Christian army marched in three divisions, with infantry ahead and probably on the flanks of the knightly cavalry, possibly with *turcopoles* in advance and further out on the flanks. According to the 13th-century *The Rule of the Templars* no one was allowed to leave their allotted place while on the march, with the squires riding ahead of the knights and the baggage bringing up the rear.

The fact that tactics soon adopted by the Crusaders in the Middle East mirrored those of Byzantium may have been a common response to a common Turco-Muslim foe, rather than a result of the Crusaders directly learning from the Byzantines. Perhaps the most immediate response was a use

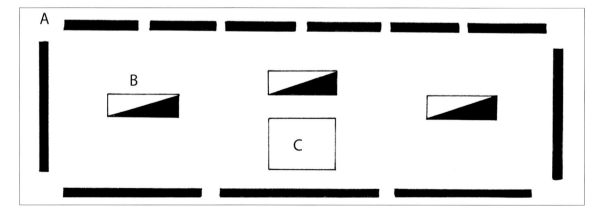

of smaller cavalry units than had been seen in the West, this giving a commander more flexibility. Even in the early 12th century these were usually sent against the enemy in sequence rather than all at once. On the other hand, smaller cavalry formations were more vulnerable if the enemy counter-attacked, particularly as more lightly armoured Muslim horsemen tended to be faster and more responsive.

Greater discipline, tactical restraint and the use of reserves also came to characterize tactics within the Crusader states, but the traditional cavalry charge remained virtually the only offensive tactic available to their armies when facing more flexible Muslim foes. On some occasions more sophisticated tactics were attempted, such as hiding a second or reserve division behind hills; but this could also fail, if the Westerners' characteristic overenthusiasm led the first division to pursue an apparently fleeing enemy, only to get itself defeated by a counter-attack before reserves

A carved ivory or bone chess piece in the form of a closely packed group of dismounted knights. (Episcopal Museum, inv. 1063, Ravenna)

had time to reach the scene. On other occasions the reserve either emerged too quickly and spoiled any chance of catching the enemy unawares, or panicked when the first division was overcome, and fled – only to be ambushed itself on the way home.

The Rule of the Templars sheds interesting light on how such knightly cavalry charges actually worked. Apparently 'brother knights' of the Order would attack in a single line of *eschielles* or squadrons, with a more densely packed formation of mounted sergeants in support, plus a guard of ten men to protect the *gonfanon* banner. Great efforts were made to keep the horses close together during the charge, and a man would be punished if he intentionally moved out of his place. If, however, a knight was unable to rejoin his own unit following a mêlée, he was instructed to make for the Marshal's banner. The function of the sergeants was to keep enemies at a distance while the knights reformed. Unarmoured men were permitted to withdraw if injured, but armoured men had to maintain their position unless specifically permitted to leave. The squires seem to have come behind the sergeants with spare horses, while the *turcopoles*, though normally operating as a separate unit, might also be distributed in support of the knights like other sergeants. Whatever the elaborate rules governing the knightly charge, it remained most effective when used against static foes – who tended to be fellow Christians.

Meanwhile, crossbowmen and other infantry were essential, both to keep enemies at bay until an opportunity came to unleash the charge, and to protect the Crusader knights if their charge had failed. As a result the Crusaders' single most important military capability was to endure prolonged harrassment, rather than actually attacking the enemy. These passive, essentially reactive tactics led to close cooperation between horse and foot. Even in the 12th century the most common Crusader battle formation appears to have been cavalry placed behind a defensive array of spear- and bow-armed infantry; although this mirrored Fatimid rather than Turkish opponents, it also reflected an existing Mediterranean European tradition, and had not been learned in the Middle East. The same idea was used in the late 12th century, with footsoldiers opening gaps in their formations through which knights could charge.

A slight variation was seen during the Third Crusade's march down the Palestinian coast, with the cavalry protected by the sea on their right and a column of infantry on their left. There was clearly nothing new about King Richard I's subsequent use of a line of infantry and dismounted knights, those with spears kneeling with their weapons thrust into the ground as pikes, while also being supported by crossbowmen, each of whom was helped by a loader. Despite the suggestion of Richard's somewhat sycophantic chronicler, this tactic had long been used by the armies of both Muslim and Crusader states.

Battle of Lake Peipus, 5 April 1242, in which forces of Novgorod under Alexander Nevskii defeated Northern Crusaders led by Bishop Hermann of Tartu. Following wide-ranging manoeuvres largely confined to areas of frozen marsh between dense forests, both sides crossed the frozen channel linking Lake Peipus with its southern extension, often called Lake Pskov.

Initial dispositions:
(**A**) Alexander Nevskii's household cavalry drawn up behind Novgorod militia; (**B**) Russian left wing; (**C**) Russian right wing, including contingent of Turco-Mongol horse-archers; (**D**) Crusader array, with Livonian feudal contingent on right, Teutonic Knights in centre, and Danish feudal forces from northern Estonia on left; (**E**) Estonian auxiliaries.

Movements: (**1**) Russian army crosses frozen lake, then adopts a defensive position at Raven's Rock; (**2**) Probable route of pursuing Crusader army across frozen lake; (**3**) Alternative Crusader route, via Piiris Island; (**4**) Crusader frontal attack forces back Novgorod militia; (**5**) Attack by Russian right, including horse-archers, hits Danes in flank, causing them to flee. They are followed by the Crusader right flank and Estonian auxiliaries, leaving the Teutonic Knights surrounded.

Nor was the effectiveness of defensive tactics disproved by the great disaster at Hattin in 1187. While it is true that on that occasion Saladin's army won control of available water-sources, and fought better in the final encounter, the Crusaders' real problems began when they changed their line of march and lost cohesion, whereupon their morale collapsed. It is also interesting to note that as the army fell apart, first the infantry, and then the cavalry, headed for a nearby hill, where they made a final defensive stand around the king's tent; only that tent's collapse marked the end of the struggle.

It seems as if several supposedly more old-fashioned methods of using the cavalry lance were readopted by Western knights when fighting Muslims in the Holy Land. Similarly, there seems to have been a limited revival in the use of the old-fashioned baldric in the 13th-century Crusader states of the Middle East, perhaps because it was suitable for fighting on foot in defensive siege warfare. Crusader cavalry élites were, by contrast, amongst the first Christian warriors to copy the long-established Middle Eastern fashion of carrying two swords, one on a belt and the other attached to the saddle. By the later 13th century European observers had become aware of the limitations imposed by traditional tactics, some of them urging Crusaders to adopt the highly disciplined formations of the Mamluk army (though they did not say how this was to be done, nor how the results should be exploited).

The troops of the Middle Eastern Crusader states were essentially the same as those of Mediterranean Europe, with the addition of *turcopole* light cavalry. Though the latter could charge in close formations with the heavy cavalry when necessary, their main role was to serve as light cavalry horse-archers. Even so, infantry crossbowmen remained even more important for all the Crusader states, whether in the Middle East or Greece following the Fourth Crusade, and the overall proportion of infantry to cavalry apparently increased throughout the 12th and 13th centuries. The crossbow's slow rate of shooting might be expected to have proved a severe disadvantage for Crusader infantry, but in practice the Muslim (and above all Turkish) tactic of separate and limited – rather than continuous – cavalry attacks tended to give the Christian footsoldiers enough time to reload.

The 'arms race' between the Turkish horseman's composite bow and the European infantryman's crossbow was, in fact, a minor epic in the history of military technology. The effective range of the 13th-century crossbow was little more than half that of the Turkish composite, but it shot a shorter, aerodynamically more efficient and potentially heavier bolt than the long, lightweight Turkish arrow. Archaeological finds have shown that by the 13th century special armour-piercing arrowheads had reached the Iberian peninsula.

There may have been a relative decline from the 12th to 14th centuries in the importance of field fortifications, which seem to feature less prominently in written sources. Nevertheless, *The Rule of the Templars* still included specific instructions on what knights and sergeants should do if such an encampment was attacked: those nearest to the threat should join in the defence, while the others should assemble around the chapel tent to await the Master's instructions.

The military theorists of the mid 13th century do not seem to have been blinded by tradition, although their ideas continued to be based upon available military technology and practices. For example, following the devastating Mongol invasion of Central Europe one such theorist suggested dealing with the Mongols' unfamiliar horse-archery harassment tactics by using massed crossbowmen. As an alternative, he suggested placing heavily armoured cavalry riding fully armoured horses in the front ranks, carrying especially large shields with which to protect their horses' heads from the Mongols' arrows. There is, however, no clear evidence that such ideas were put into practice.

BIBLIOGRAPHY

Abels, R., 'From Alfred to Harold II: The Military Failure of the Late Anglo-Saxon State', in R. Abels & B.S. Bachrach (eds), *The Normans and their Adversaries in War* (Woodbridge, 2001)

Airaldi, G., 'The Genoese Art of Warfare', in D.A. Agius & I.R. Netton (eds), *Across the Mediterranean Frontiers: Trade, Politics and Religion, 650–1450* (Turnhout, 1997)

Bachrach, B.S., 'Charles Martel, Mounted Shock Combat, the Stirrup and Feudalism', *Studies in Medieval and Renaissance History*, 7 (1970)

Bachrach, B.S., 'The Feigned Retreat at Hastings', *Medieval Studies*, 33 (1971); also in S. Morillo (ed), *The Battle of Hastings: Sources and Interpretations* (Woodbridge, 1996)

Beeler, J., *Warfare in England 1066–1189* (Ithaca, 1966)

Beeler, J., *Warfare in Feudal Europe, 730–1200* (Ithaca, 1971)

Bennett, M., 'La Règle du Temple as a military manual, or how to deliver a cavalry charge', in C. Harper-Bill et al (eds), *Studies in Medieval History presented to R. Allen Brown* (Woodbridge, 1989)

Bennett, M., 'The Myth of the Military Supremacy of Knightly Cavalry', in M. Strickland (ed), *Armies, Chivalry and Warfare in Medieval Britain and France, Harlaxton Medieval Studies VII* (London, 1998)

Bowlus, C.R., 'Tactical and Strategic Weaknesses of Horse Archers on the Eve of the First Crusade', in M. Balard (ed), *Autour de la Première Croisade* (Paris, 1996)

Contamine, P. (trans M. Jones), *War in the Middle Ages* (Oxford, 1984)

Cook, D.R., 'The Norman military revolution in England', *Battle Conference on Anglo-Norman Studies, Proceedings*, 1 (1978)

Ekdahl, S., 'Horses and Crossbows: Two Important Warfare Advantages of the Teutonic Order in Prussia', in H. Nicholson (ed), *The Military Orders, Vol. 2: Welfare and Warfare* (Aldershot, 1998)

Flori, J., 'Encore l'usage de la lance... La technique du combat chevaleresque vers l'an 1100', *Cahiers de Civilizations Médiévales*, 31 (1988)

France, J., *Western Warfare in the Age of the Crusades 1000–1300* (New York, 1999)

García Fitz, F., *Castilla y León Frente al Islam. Estrategias de Expansión y Tácticas Militares (Siglos XI–XIII)* (Seville, 1998)

Gillingham, J., 'Up with Orthodoxy!: In Defense of Vegetian Warfare', *The Journal of Medieval Military History*, 2 (2004)

A rare example of a single-edged Viking sword; Iceland, probably early 11th century. (National Museum of Iceland, on loan to Reykjavik Airport Display; author's photograph)

Griffith, P., *The Viking Art of War* (London, 1995)

Hatto, A.T., 'Archery and Chivalry: A Noble Prejudice', *Modern Language Review*, 35 (1940)

Hooper, N., 'Anglo-Saxon Warfare on the Eve of the Conquest; A Brief Survey', *Proceedings of the Battle Conference on Anglo-Norman Studies*, 1 (1978)

Lindner, R.P., 'Nomadism, Horses and Huns', *Past and Present*, 92 (1981)

Lot. F., *L'Art Militaire et les Armées du Moyen Age en Europe et dans le Proche Orient* (Paris, 1946)

Marshall, C.J., *Warfare in the Latin East, 1192–1291* (Cambridge, 1992)

Meschini, M., *Battaglie Medievali* (Milan, 2005)

Mitchell, R., 'Light Cavalry, Heavy Cavalry, Horse Archers, Oh My! What Abstract Definitions Don't Tell Us About 1205 Adrianople', *The Journal of Medieval Military History*, 6 (2008)

Morillo, S., 'The "Age of Cavalry" Revisited', in D.J. Kagay & L.J.A. Villalon (eds), *The Circle of War in the Middle Ages* (Woodbridge, 1999)

Nicolle, D., *Crusader Warfare, Vol. 1: Byzantium, Western Europe and the Battle for the Holy Land* (London, 2007)

Pieri, P., 'Alcune quistioni sopre la fanteria in Italia nel periodo comunale', *Rivista Storica Italiana*, 50 (1933)

Richard, J., 'Les causes des victoires Mongoles d'après les historiens occidentaux du XIIIe siècle', *Central Asiatic Journal*, 23 (1979)

Rogers, C.J., 'The Vegetian "Science of Warfare" in the Middle Ages', *The Journal of Medieval Military History*, 1 (2002)

Ross, D.J.A., 'L'Originalité de Turoldus: le maniement de la lance', *Cahiers de Civilizations Médiévale*, 6 (1963)

Settia, A.A., 'Infantry and Cavalry in Lombardy (11th–12th Centuries)', *The Journal of Medieval Military History*, 6 (2008)

Soler del Campo, A., 'Sistemas de Combate en la Iconografia Mozarabe y Andalusi Altomedieval', *Boletín de la Asociación Española de Orientalistas*, 22 (1986)

Strickland, M., 'Securing the North: Invasion and the Strategy of Defence in Twelfth-Century Anglo-Scottish Warfare', *Anglo-Norman Studies*, 12 (1990)

Verbruggen, J.F. (trans K. DeVries), 'The Role of Cavalry in Medieval Warfare', *The Journal of Medieval Military History*, 3 (2005)

Verbruggen, J.F., *The Art of Warfare in Western Europe during the Middle Ages* (Oxford, 1977)

Zouache, A., *Armées et Combats en Syria (491/1098-569/1174)* (Damascus, 2008)

Surviving pieces of medieval 'soft armour' are exceptionally rare. The so-called 'Sleeve of St Martin' in a church near Paris is probably part of a 13th-century medieval *aketon* or *gambeson*. ('*Manche de St Martin*' in parish church, Bussy-St-Martin; photograph Y. Bourhis, Conseil general de Seine-et-Marne)

INDEX

References to illustrations are shown in **bold**.
Plates are shown with page locators in brackets.

'African drill' 12
Age of Migrations 5–6, 10–12
'Alan drill' 12
Alans 10, 13, 31
Alemanni 14
ambush tactic 12, 14, 36, 45, 48
Anglo-Saxons 17, 22, 29–31, 37–38, 48
  archers 52
  Battle of Brémule (1119) **E** (34, 35)
  Battle of Catraeth (AD 600) **A** (10, 11)
  Battle of Hastings (1066) **D** (30, 31), **38,
    39, 40**
  Battle of the Standard (1138) **44**
  field fortifications 37
  infantry 31
  'shield-wall/shield-fort' tactics **B** (18, 19), 31
Arab-Andalusian saddles 26
archers 13, 32–33, 41–42, 50–52, 61
  Carolingians 33
  Celts 33
  Germanic armies 14
  Huns 13
  Iberian armies 33
  Magyar-Hungarians **C** (22, 23), 33, 34, 37
  Normans 33, 41, 52
  Romans 12, **13**, 19, 33
  Sassanians 19, **C** (22, 23)
  Scandinavians 38
  Vikings 33
Avars 10, 14, 26
axes 22, **D** (30, 31)

Basques 15
Berber saddles 26
bows and arrows 12, 14, 15, 19, 32–33, 52
Brémule, Battle of (1119) **E** (34, 35)
Britain 22–23 *see also* Anglo-Saxons
  Battle of Catraeth (AD 600) **A** (10, 11)
  field fortifications 24
  post-Roman 16–17
  'shield-wall/shield-fort' tactics **B** (18, 19)
Bulgarian armies 28–29
Byzantines *see* Romans

camel-mounted infantry 8
Carcano, Battle of (1160) 50
Carolingians 24, **27, 28, 29, 32,** 33–34
  ambush tactic 36
  archers 33
  cuneus formations 28
  field fortifications 33
Catraeth, Battle of (AD 600) **A** (10, 11)
cattle-rustling 48
cavalry/infantry combinations 48–55
Celts 16–17, 47–48
  archers 33
  Battle of Catraeth (AD 600) **A** (10, 11)
  infantry 55
chain mail **4, 5**
Châlons, Battle of (AD 451) 10, 21
Civitate, Battle of (1053) **36**
clothing
  chain mail **4, 5**
  helmets **4, 5, 6, 16, 32, 43**
  soft armour **33, 63**
crossbows 24, 41, 41–42, 50, **G** (50, 51), 52,
  H (54, 55), 61
Crusades 5, 45, 47, 57, 57–62, 58

dawn attacks 17
discipline 9, 39
disguise, as a tactic 16

ditch-traps 16, 38
duels 29

espionage 40

feigned flight tactic 12, 13, 15, 41, 45
field fortifications 20, 21, 24, 33, 36, 37, 38, 49,
  G (50, 51), 61
formations 12, 14, 20–21, 58, 59
  conrois formation **E** (34, 35), 41, 42, **F** (46, 47)
  cuneus formation 10, 15, **C** (22, 23), 28
  phalanx formation **F** (46, 47)
  schiltron formation 55
'four-horned' saddles 19
France 33, 39–41, 42–45
  archers 50–52
  Battle of Brémule (1119) **E** (34, 35)
Franks 14–15, 16, 22

Germanic armies 14–16, 34–36, 45
  Battle of Legnano (1176) **F** (46, 47), 49–50
  Battle of Taginae (AD 552) **14**
  Battle of the Lech (AD 955) **C** (22, 23)
  field fortifications 21–22
Guadalete, Battle of (AD 711) **25**
guerrilla tactics 17, 22, 40, 45–47

Hastings, Battle of (1066) **D** (30, 31), **38, 39,** 40–41
helmets **4, 5, 6, 16, 32, 43**
horses
  armour 12, **21,** 27, **G** (50, 51), **52**
  saddles 17, 19, 20, **25,** 26–27
  stirrups 20, 24–26
horseshoes 26
hostage taking 40
Huns 7, 10, 13, 21

Iberian armies 27, 29, 33, 38–39, 55–57
infantry 48–52, **G** (50, 51), 60
  Alans 13
  Anglo-Saxons 31
  British armies 16, 17
  Celts 55
  Franks 16
  Germanic armies 15
  Huns 13
  Italy 45
  Ottonians 34
  Romans 8, 9, 20–24
'Italian drill' 12
Italy 36, 49–50 *see also* Lombards; Romans
  archers 33
  Battle of Civitate (1053) **36**
  formations **F** (46, 47)
  infantry 45

javelins **A** (10, 11), 13, 14, 16, **26,** 49

Lake Peipus, Battle of (1242) 60
lances 5, 19, 28, **D** (30, 31), 41, 42, 61
Las Navas de Tolosa, Battle of (1212) **G** (50, 51)
Lech, Battle of the (AD 955) **C** (22, 23)
Legnano, Battle of (1176) **F** (46, 47), 49–50
Lombards 15, 16
  Battle of Carcano (1160) 50
  Battle of Civitate (1053) **36**
  Battle of Legnano (1176) **F** (46, 47), 49–50
  Battle of Taginae (AD 552) **14**
longbows 32–33, 52

Magyar-Hungarian armies 24, **32,** 36–37
  archers 33, 34, 37
  Battle of the Lech (AD 955) **C** (22, 23)
  field fortifications 36
Muret, Battle of (1213) 58

Normans 5, 39–41, 42–45, 48
  archers 33, 41, 52
  Battle of Brémule (1119) **E** (34, 35)
  Battle of Civitate (1053) **36**
  Battle of Hastings (1066) **D** (30, 31), **38, 39,**
    40–41
  Battle of the Standard (1138) **44**
Ostrogoths 14, **14,** 15
Ottonians 34–36

Pelagonia, Battle of (1259) **H** (54, 55)
Polish armies 37, 47, 53

Romans 5–12, 16–17, **17,** 20, 27, 28, **31,** 32–33, 37
  archers 12, **13,** 19, 33
  Battle of Catraeth (AD 600) **A** (10, 11)
  Battle of Châlons (AD 451) 10, 21
  Battle of Pelagonia (1259) **H** (54, 55)
  Battle of Taginae (AD 552) **14**
  fighting on horseback 17–20
  infantry **8, 9,** 20–24
Russian armies 36

saddles 17, 19, 20, 25, 26–27
Saladin's army 61
Sassanians 7, 15, 19, **C** (22, 23)
Scandinavia 38, 52
Scottish armies **44,** 47, 55
'Scythian drill' 12
'shield-wall/shield-fort' tactics **B** (18, 19), 21, 31,
  37, 38
shields **A** (10, 11), 13, 14, 15, 19, 22, 24, **43**
'shock' tactics 44–45
'shower-shooting,' archers **C** (22, 23)
sieges 24, 39, 42, 57
Slavs 14, 28–29, 34, 36, 37, 52–53
Spanish armies 38–39, **40**
spears **A** (10, 11), 15, 16, 17–19, 29
Standard, Battle of the (1138) **44**
steppe peoples 5, 6, 10, 12–14, 20, 21
stirrups 20, 24–26
supply lines, attacking 27, 42
swords 13, **26, 62**

Taginae, Battle of (AD 552) **14**
throwing axes 22, **D** (30, 31)
Thuringians 16
turnafuye tactics 29

Umayyads 25

Vandals 14
Vikings 24, 31–32, 37–38
  archers 33
  field fortifications 33, 38
  'shield-wall/shield-fort' tactics **B** (18, 19)
Visigoths 14, 15, **15,** 16
  Battle of Châlons (AD 451) 10, 21
  Battle of Guadalete (AD 711) **25**

wagons, as field fortifications 20, 21, 36
weapons 8, **A** (10, 11) *see also* shields
  bows and arrows 12, 14, 15, 19, 32–33, 52
  crossbows 24, 41, 41–42, 50, **G** (50, 51), 52,
    H (54, 55), 61
  javelins 13, 14, 16, **26,** 49
  lances 5, 19, 28, **D** (30, 31), 41, 42, 61
  spears 15, 16, 17–19, 29
  swords 13, **26, 62**
  throwing axes 22, **D** (30, 31)
Welsh armies 48, 55
wooden-framed saddles 17, 20, **25**

Zallaqa, Battle of (1086) **40**